MICROSCOPY
for Students

J. D. CASARTELLI

McGraw-Hill Publishing Company Limited
LONDON
New York · Toronto · Sydney

Published by
McGraw-Hill Publishing Company Limited
McGraw-Hill House, Maidenhead, Berkshire, England

94012

THIS BOOK HAS BEEN SET IN MONOPHOTO TIMES NEW ROMAN 10 ON 12 POINT
AND PRINTED AND BOUND IN GREAT BRITAIN BY
WILLIAM CLOWES AND SONS LIMITED, LONDON AND BECCLES

Preface

During the past 32 years I have been, through my position as a technical representative of W. Watson & Sons Ltd., in constant association with microscope workers in all fields—medical schools, hospitals, technical colleges, schools, industrial laboratories and research establishments and University departments—and, in addition, I have lectured to and taken classes in microscopy for various scientific bodies, students, and, in particular, members of the Institute of Medical Laboratory Technology who have been preparing for their examinations.

During this time there has been a constant stream of questions on the use, selection of, and reasons for particular microscopes, accessories and techniques. This book has been written to provide the answers to many of these questions of routine microscopy, and to give some preliminary information on the use of special equipment for some of the newer techniques. It is not intended as a treatise on the microscope as a whole, nor on microscopy as a subject, nor on any of the special new techniques. Other books exist which cover these aspects in full, and the reader is referred to these books if the subject is to be studied further after the introductory information in this book has been assimilated.

In writing the book I have had in mind, in particular, the current syllabus for the courses and examinations of the Institute of Medical Laboratory Technology, and many of the microscopy questions in these examinations are answered under the appropriate headings in the book. However, it is hoped that its scope is broad enough to serve, not only as a textbook for these special courses, but also as an explanatory book and a reference book for all users of the microscope in their early stages. It may well be of help to students in universities and colleges in their introductory period in biology, and as a reference book in laboratories in hospitals and industrial establishments.

I am grateful to Professor N. F. Robertson, of the Department of Botany, University of Hull, for reading my manuscript and for writing the Foreword to this book.

I gladly acknowledge the help which I have received from my late firm, W. Watson & Sons Ltd., for permission to quote from their literature, and for the use of some of their illustrations for Figs. 1, 2, 3, 4, 5, 16, 18, 19, 20, 21, 22, 38, 39, 40, 41 and 42.

In addition, I acknowledge the permission of J. & A. Churchill Ltd., for the use of illustrations, Figs. 29, 30, 31, 32, 33 and 34 in the Text, which are based on Wredden, "The Microscope" (1947) Churchill; and the permission of Mr. L. Platts, of the Pathology Department, University of Sheffield, for the photograph for Fig. 35.

J. D. CASARTELLI

Poynton, 1965

Foreword

Teaching students how to use the microscope is one of the primary duties of a University teacher of biology; finding time to reinforce and extend this teaching is one of his difficulties. This book is a source to which technicians, undergraduates and research students and their teachers can refer for practical instruction and simple theoretical treatment. In my experience exponents of microscope technique fall into two categories, the direct and the esoteric. The first allow no frills, they have a routine which they demand should be followed like an army drill. The second, from their deeper knowledge have reservations about methods and a critical appreciation of performance, but they can be frightening to the beginner. There are great microscopists like Dr. John Baker and Professor Robert Barer, who have expounded their expertise without instilling fear or confusion. It is none the less refreshing to have this handbook, from an author who knows microscopes and microscopists in a way that is peculiarly his own. He has used the instruments and supplied them, repaired them, demonstrated them, taught about them and enjoyed them. He has seen the ignorance of many biologists and known the expertise of others. All this is clear from the pages of this book where one can almost see the instruments he describes and feel the shame of the poor performance and one can feel too the satisfaction of the best. The author's practical understanding of the problems of the manufacturer and user is abundantly clear and he continues to expound these against a background of simplified theory which is sufficient yet satisfactory.

Mr. Casartelli's many friends will welcome this book as they welcomed him on his visits to them, because they liked him and profited from him. I commend this book to all beginners in microscopy and to all those, not beginners, who feel some insecurity about their comprehension of the potentialities of the instrument they use.

N. F. ROBERTSON

Professor of Botany,
University of Hull.

Table of Contents

PART 1

General Microscopy

CHAPTER 1

The Microscope Stand

The stand is essentially a mechanical frame to carry the optical system of the instrument. As there are three basic optical units—the eyepiece, the objective and the condenser—the stand must carry these in rigid relation to each other without vibration or distortion of the optical axis which runs through all three units and, at the same time, it must be provided with adjusting mechanism whereby the distances between the three units can be varied at will with the utmost accuracy. In addition, the platform which carries the specimen must hold it strictly at right angles to the optical axis.

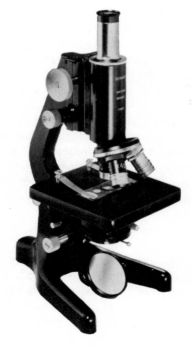

Fig. 1. Monocular microscope

Taking, first of all, the older forms of instruments, the stand consists of a *foot*, usually of horse-shoe shape provided with three contact pads on the underside to give a stable support on surfaces which might not be truly flat, and of sufficient spread to provide balance and stability with the microscope in the inclined position.

To this foot is hinged the main member, the *limb*, which carries the three optical units and the focusing mechanism and, through the hinged joint, provision for inclining the limb towards the user. The limb carries, also, the *stage* on which rests the specimen, and the *body* which has at its lower end the mounting for the objectives, usually a *rotating nosepiece* or other objective changer, and, at its upper end, the eyepiece. In some instruments there is provision for altering the distance between objective and eyepiece by means of the *draw-tube* within the body.

Focusing adjustments to raise or lower the body in relation to the stage are provided, two speeds of adjustment being available, known as the fast or *coarse adjustment* and the slow or *fine adjustment*.

Below the stage is the mounting for the condenser, called the *substage*, and, except in the most elementary instruments, there is provision made for altering the distance between the condenser and the stage by some form of focusing mechanism. Finally, at the bottom of the limb is mounted the *mirror*.

In recent times there have been changes in the design of the stand.

The coarse and fine adjustment controls have been moved to a position below the stage and they are frequently co-axial. The inclination of the limb has been omitted by fixing the limb to the foot or base, and the necessary inclination is provided by an inclined mounting for the eyepiece. In place of the mirror, which requires an external illuminant, the base usually carries the illumination built into it.

Further, whereas in earlier instruments the coarse and fine adjustments moved the body in relation to the fixed stage, more recent models move the stage in relation to the fixed body, or, in at least one make, the focusing mechanism is divided, so that the coarse adjustment moves the body in relation to the stage while the fine adjustment moves the stage in relation to the body. This latter construction is probably the more satisfactory in that the comparatively long and frequent movement in coarse adjustment is taken away from the stage thus reducing the chance of early wear, for while the stage must move for focusing, it must retain its strict position at right angles to the optical axis.

Fig. 2. Student microscope with built-in illumination

It is necessary to discuss some of these parts of the microscope in greater detail, as follows:

Coarse Adjustment

This movement is usually derived from a rack and pinion system which is provided with diagonal teeth. This ensures that one or more teeth of the pinion are engaged with those of the rack thereby giving a smooth, continuous motion free from "chatter" or jerky movement. Because the teeth are carefully shaped to ensure smooth engagement, care must be taken to prevent damage to these teeth by misuse (see Chapter 6).

Fine Adjustment

This movement frequently originates in a screw and nut mechanism. The screw is of very fine pitch, about 70 threads to the inch, which enables a very slow movement when the screw is rotated. The movement of the screw or of the nut actuates a lever with arms of unequal length, giving a movement which is a 5:1 reduction of that of the screw or nut. The result of this is a very small movement of the objective (or of the stage) for one turn of the control head of the fine adjustment.

Figure 3 shows one such system, in which the screw, turning through a fixed nut, moves a disc which is integral with the screw,

The action of the Fine Adjustment. B—The Lever. A—The Block which is attached to the Fine Adjustment Slide. C—The Travelling Wheel that imparts the movement, actuated by the screw on the right, which is revolved by the milled heads. The reverse movement is assisted by a spring.

Fig. 3. Fine adjustment mechanism

against one arm of the lever. The other arm bears on a block which is attached to the slide carrying the body. In a typical example one revolution of the control head gives a focusing movement of 0·005 in. or 0·12 mm.

In a well designed instrument, the slides of both coarse and fine adjustments are provided with means to take up wear as it occurs, and the tension on the spindle of the pinion is also adjustable.

Draw-Tube

The draw-tube is not necessary for much routine and student work and is, therefore, frequently omitted, the distance between objective and eyepiece (called the *tube length*) being fixed at an optimum distance. There are, however, certain techniques (micrometry, for instance) and critical microscopy (cover-glass thickness correction) where the draw-tube is essential. The draw-tube is engraved with calibration lines and figures so that the exact tube length can be ascertained.

Objective Changer

This is usually a rotating turret or nosepiece carrying up to four objectives, with an indexing spring mechanism to ensure that when the nosepiece is rotated, each objective is brought into position so that its optical axis coincides with that of the microscope. To keep the objectives clean, the rotating nosepiece must be dustproof.

As an alternative to the rotating nosepiece there can be found the sliding objective carrier which slides into a fixed frame at the bottom of the body. Each objective is provided with its own carrier, and each carrier is provided with adjustable stops for the accurate positioning of the optical axis. This system works perfectly provided that the fitting does not become loose due to wear, and provided that the sliding fitting parts are kept clean from particles of dirt or grit which would not only promote rapid wear but also affect the position of the optical axis of the objective.

The Substage

The mounting of the condenser depends on the quality of the optics of the condenser. For the simplest types, such as the Abbe, where the unit, due to its various optical short-comings, is insensitive to precise centring and focusing (as will be discussed in a later chapter) a simple sleeve fitting in the substage to accept the condenser assembly is sufficient.

But with more advanced condensers there must be some centring adjustment, either on the substage or on the condenser mount for the precise centring of the optical axis of the condenser with that of the rest of the microscope, with, of course, adequate means of focusing the condenser.

The substage or the condenser mount must have an iris diaphragm to control the aperture at which the condenser is working, and, preferably, a removable holder for filters or diffuser.

2

The Mirror

In microscopes provided for external illumination, the mirror is frequently double-sided. One side is concave and the other plain. It is a rule in good microscopy that the plain mirror must be used whenever a condenser is used in the substage. This is because the condenser is designed to focus light from a distance—i.e. nearly parallel rays—on to the specimen. If, however, the concave mirror is used with a condenser, the mirror converges the light before it reaches the condenser which then converges it still further and, strictly speaking, this double convergence prevents accurate focusing of the light on to the specimen. In view of this, it is becoming customary to omit the concave mirror in routine and student microscopes and so remove the likelihood of improper setting-up. There are exceptions to this which will be discussed in Chapter 4.

In microscopes with built-in illumination the mirror is, of course, omitted altogether. The illuminant with its own condenser lens is accurately positioned on the optical axis of the microscope.

The Stage

In the elementary or simplest student microscope, the stage is known as a plain stage. It is a square or rectangular plate, of great rigidity, with an optically flat top surface on which the specimen rests, and it is usually treated with a reagent-resisting finish. Most stages are large enough to accommodate a Petri dish. Spring clips are provided to keep the specimen in firm contact with the stage surface and yet allow movement of the specimen by sliding it with finger pressure for location and searching. With the stage clips removed, the specimen is free to slide over the stage in every direction so that the clips are necessary if the stage is inclined. Many microscopists consider it good practice to learn delicate finger control so that the specimen can be moved smoothly and for very small distances even under high magnification.

However, in much work, especially at high magnification, finger control can be both laborious and inaccurate, especially if systematic searching of the whole of a specimen is involved. To make this easier and more accurate, the *mechanical stage* is provided, either as an attachment to a plain stage, or built-in to the microscope. By means of sensitive controls—screw, rack and pinion, or worm and nut mechanisms—the specimen can be moved slowly and evenly so that every part of it can be brought into the field of view of an objective. The controls move the specimen to and from the observer (frequently described as North–South movement) and also from side to side (East–West movement) and the range of movement should be enough to bring every part of a standard 3 in. × 1 in. slide under the objective. The control heads are frequently found to be co-axial, projecting from the side of the stage, or hanging downwards below it, or, in a few cases, located above the stage. However arranged, the controls should be capable of moving the specimen

Fig. 4. Mechanical stage

slowly and evenly and without lost motion, or backlash, on reversal of the movement of the control head.

For certain purposes, e.g. in the petrological microscope, and for photomicrography, the stage is provided with an additional motion —rotation with centring adjustments. This enables the specimen to be rotated in relation to either the polarizer and analyser of the polarizing microscope, or to the plate or film-frame in photomicrography.

Scales and Verniers

Most mechanical stages are fitted with two scales and verniers— one running North and South, the other East and West. It should be clearly understood that the purpose of these is not for use as a measuring device—the fact that, to make them easily readable, the lines are engraved with considerable thickness would prevent any accuracy in measurement. They are to be used as a position finding device.

Suppose that a particular part of a specimen is of such interest that it might have to be examined again and again. As the amount of the specimen covered by the field of view of an objective is extremely small compared with the whole specimen, random searching for the particular field desired can be laborious and time-wasting. If, however, on finding a point of interest, the readings of both of the scales and verniers be recorded, and the position of the slide label (left or right) be noted, then, provided that the same microscope be used again, pre-setting of the scales and verniers to the recorded setting, and mounting of the slide with the label in the noted position ought to bring the particular point of interest at least partially into the field of view.

The method of reading scales and verniers is sometimes not fully understood. The *main scale* has a series of lines at intervals of 1 mm with appropriate figures for identification. It will be noted that the *vernier* is a short scale with ten lines and figures, and, moreover, that the length of the ten lines of the vernier correspond exactly to nine divisions of the main scale. In use, the reading point is the *zero line* of the vernier. If for example, it is found that this zero line lies between, say, 14 and 15 on the main scale, it means that we have more than 14 but less than 15 to record, and the first part of our recording will, therefore, be 14.

The vernier is now examined, and it will be found that one of the vernier lines will coincide more or less exactly with one of the lines of the main scale—all the other vernier lines will be slightly separate from a main scale line. We note the number of the vernier line which is in closest coincidence, say number 7 line, and this gives us the decimal in our complete recording, which will read 14·7.

If this procedure is carried out for both North and South and East and West scales, we finish up with two numbers and decimals, and we note the position of the label of the slide.

To find this field of view on a subsequent occasion, we select the same objective; place the slide on the stage with the label to the left or right, as recorded, and then preset both scales and verniers to the recorded figures. This should locate the specimen so that the desired field is now in view.

Binocular Heads

While it is still standard practice to provide the student microscope with a monocular head only, increasing use is being made of the binocular head, particularly when long periods of work with the microscope have to be undertaken. This is to prevent fatigue which follows from the continuous use of one eye. So serious can this fatigue be that, apart from the discomfort, inflammation of the eye, headache, etc., to the user, an overworked eye becomes incapable of registering what it actually sees. For example, in the early days of the National Health Service, blood counting was frequently performed with monocular instruments. With the great increase in blood-counts following the introduction of the N.H.S. it was soon noticed that blood counters were reporting inaccurately after a period of work on a monocular instrument. In fact, as a test,

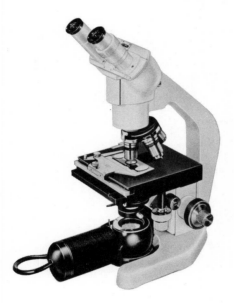

Fig. 5. Binocular microscope

a blood film would be counted in the morning when the operator was fresh, and the same film, unknown to the operator, would be introduced again in the late afternoon, and a different count would then be reported. This was entirely due to eye fatigue, and, thereafter, the binocular microscope became compulsory for this kind of work.

In the binocular microscope, the image formed by the objective is doubled by a beam-splitting prism and presented to each eye through two further prisms and the two eyepieces. It should be noted that, on emerging from the beam-splitting prism, the two light paths are at different levels. Accordingly, the two side prisms are at the same different levels, but the lengths of the light paths from the underside of the beam-splitting prism to each eyepiece are exactly the same in total, hence there is no change in magnification as between one side and the other, such as would occur if one path were longer than the other. The images thus presented are exactly

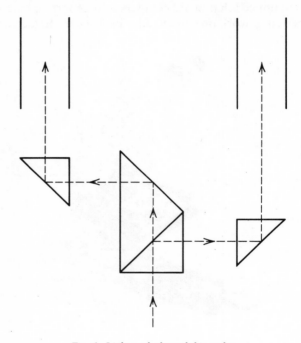

Fig. 6. Light path through binocular

the same, thus differing from the stereoscopic microscopes, discussed in Chapter 13.

In using the binocular body, the user must set the eyepieces, by the adjustment provided, to the exact interpupillary distance of his own eyes. There is usually a scale provided to indicate this interpupillary distance in millimetres. If the distance for an individual be known, he can pre-set the eyepieces by the scale before commencing work.

If the user has any optical difference between his eyes and does not wear spectacles to correct the fault, one of the eyepiece tubes is provided with an adjustment for change of focus. The microscope is focused through the side without the adjustment, keeping the other eye closed. This eye is now opened and, if the specimen is not focused as sharply as for the other eye, the adjustment of the eyepiece tube is altered until this has been achieved. Note, however, that this adjustment cannot correct for the eye defect known as astigmatism. For this, proper correcting lenses in spectacles should be worn.

CHAPTER 2

The Objective

Of the three basic optical units of the microscope—the eyepiece, the objective and the condenser—the objective is, by far, the most important. It is an indisputable fact that a microscope is only as good as its objective for it is the objective which produces the magnified image of the object and which shows all the detail, structure and general appearance from which all observations are made.

Identification

For uniformity in teaching, in discussion and in scientific literature, certain systems of identifying and naming objectives must be understood. The oldest system is by the focal length, expressed in either English measurement or in metric. *Focal length* is the distance from an object on which the objective is focused to some point within the objective and it is not, therefore, a distance which can be readily seen and measured by the user.

Recently, most workers were using the *magnification* of the objective in naming and describing it. Still more recently, and coming into use more widely, is a system of *colour coding*, in which bands of various colours on the objective mounting differentiate one objective from another.

Focal Length and Working Distance

Confusion often exists between these two terms. Focal length as described above, is of less practical importance to the user than working distance which is the distance between an object and the front lens of an objective when the latter is correctly focused. The working distance is always much less than the focal length, as will be seen from the table, p. 22, and it is this fact which may lead to trouble. At the lower magnifications this does not matter, but with objectives of focal length of 4 mm or less, the short working distance can be of great importance. For instance, as the 4 mm objective has a working distance of only 1 mm, difficulty can arise when working through the thick cover-glasses sometimes supplied with blood counting chambers. In fact, cover-glasses over 1 mm thick can be encountered, in which cases the front lens of the objective will come into contact with the cover before the under-lying blood cells can be focused.

Again, and perhaps more importantly, the 2 mm objective has a working distance of only 0·12 mm—about the thickness of a piece of writing paper—within which short distance all the final focusing has to be done. With this very short working distance it is very easy to bring the front lens into hard contact with the specimen, in which case the front lens is either scratched or actually displaced backwards off its seating. It should be realized that this front lens is a hyperhemisphere and can be mounted only by a narrow metal bezel, reinforced by cement, around the equator of the lens. Dis-placement alters the distance between the front lens and the follow-ing lens elements and, further, allows immersion oil, in which all these objectives must operate, to penetrate what should be an air space behind the front lens. Both of these happenings completely spoil the functioning of the objective which must go back to the maker for expensive repairs. Further, the specimen slide can fre-quently be broken in such an accident.

Spring-Loaded Objectives

In view of the dangers just described, it is becoming common for both 4 mm and 2 mm objectives to have their lens systems spring-mounted within the body of the objective. Should pressure be applied, by accident, to the front lens, the lens is pushed back into the body of the objective against spring pressure, and thus, much major damage is avoided. On release of the pressure on the lens, the spring returns the assembly to its normal position.

It is dangerous to assume that every microscope is equipped with this safety device, particularly with older instruments. Every stu-dent ought to be taught proper and delicate control of focusing with high power objectives without reliance on spring-loading, so that he can use any microscope without causing damage.

Parfocalled Objectives

In modern microscopes it is customary to find that the objectives are parfocalled. This term signifies that, if any one objective is focused on to the object, any other objective can be brought into use by rotating the nosepiece or using the sliding objective changer and the new objective should be found to be almost in focus, within a small touch of the fine adjustment control. An instrument is sometimes criticized as having its objectives not parfocalled when, in fact, they are correctly adjusted. The error can arise if the original focusing is done through a very low-power objective, such as the 40 mm scanner objective. These low-power objectives have considerable depth of focus and it is quite possible to do the initial focusing at either the top or the bottom of the depth of field, resulting in an apparent error when higher powers are brought into use. A useful way of checking the accuracy of parfocalling is to focus the highest powered dry objective, and then check the focus of the progressively lower powers. One would not, of course, include any oil-immersion objective in any parfocalling check, as, in use, the oil-immersion objective must be raised well above the specimen after the dry objectives have been employed, so that the immersion oil can be applied to the specimen.

Magnification

One of the prime purposes of the objective is to produce an image of an object magnified many times, and there are a number of terms relating to magnification which should be understood:

Nominal and Tube-Length. This is the magnification engraved on the body of an objective, e.g. × 40, but, as it is associated with the tube-length of the microscope, i.e. the distance between the objective and the eyepiece, it should be expressed as " × 40 (or whatever objective is being described) at a tube-length of so much". In fact, the nominal magnification is correct at only one tube-length, the optimum selected by the maker and as indicated either on the objective itself or, more usually, in the chart of magnifications in the cabinet of the microscope. If used at a longer tube-length than standard, the nominal magnification is increased by the ratio of the new tube-length to the old tube-length, and vice versa. Thus, for an objective corrected to give a nominal magnification of × 40 at a tube-length of 160 mm, use at any other (new) tube-length will modify the nominal magnification thus:

$$40 \times \frac{\text{new tube-length (mm)}}{160}$$

Particularly in examinations, and preferably in all literature, the nominal magnification should always be expressed in terms of the tube-length at which it is being used.

Manufacturers have standardized the tube-lengths at which their objectives perform best and for which they have been calculated. All British and American makers use 160 mm.

All Continental, Russian and Japanese makers use 170 mm.

The tube-length in microscopes without a draw-tube is set for the optimum distance by the length of the body and that of the eye-piece tube. In microscopes with draw-tubes, the tube-length is engraved on the outside of the draw-tube which can be withdrawn from the body until the desired line coincides with the top of the body proper from which the draw-tube is being extended.

Primary. Primary magnification of a microscope is the magnification produced by the objective itself, and it is the same as the nominal magnification provided that the standard tube-length is being employed.

Total. The total magnification of a microscope is that seen by the user when looking through the eyepiece. It is the product of the primary magnification and that of the eyepiece. E.g. objective × 40, eyepiece × 10; Total magnification = × 400.

Useful. Useful magnification is the total magnification of a microscope when it does not exceed a certain amount which is imposed by the numerical aperture (see p. 20) of the objective.

For all objectives of the achromatic type the limit is set at 1000 times the numerical aperture (N.A. × 1000), while for more highly developed objectives of the fluorite and apochromatic types the limit is set at about 1500 times the numerical aperture (N.A. × 1500). Within these limits, the detail in an objective increases as the magnification is raised, hence the term Useful Magnification.

Empty. Empty magnification means the using of a total magnification in excess of the above limits. Under these conditions, increasing the magnification is accompanied by a progressive loss of detail despite the most careful focusing.

By Calculation. It sometimes happens that an older objective is marked with only its focal length and without any indication of its magnification. There is a method whereby the magnification of the objective can be calculated, bearing in mind that this is associated with the tube-length at which it is being used. If the tube-length, in millimetres, is divided by the focal length of the objective, expressed in millimetres, the result is the magnification of the objective. For example: an objective of 16 mm focal length used at a tube-length of 160 mm has a magnification of × 10.

$$\frac{160}{16} = \times 10$$

This holds true for all objectives except the 2 mm. If the above calculation is made for this objective, the result is × 80, whereas most 2 mm objectives are marked × 100. The discrepancy is due to the fact that in this objective 2 mm is to be regarded rather as a type name than as a precise measurement of focal length. In actual fact, these objectives have focal lengths of less than 2 mm, usually 1·6 mm, which, under the above rule would produce × 100, but it would be rather confusing to read of objectives of focal lengths of, say, 1·5 mm, 1·6 mm or 1·7 mm, all of them being for all practical purposes, the same objective. Thus it has become customary to refer to all objectives of this order of magnification as of focal length 2 mm. But, apart from this one power of objective, the rule holds good.

Objectives: Dry, Water-Immersion and Oil-Immersion

All objectives are calculated to work through some specific medium—air, water or oil—and they are designated dry, water-immersion and oil-immersion respectively. To understand why there are these differences some consideration must be given to what happens to light when it passes from one medium to another.

Let us suppose that light is travelling in glass and then emerges into air. From Fig. 7 it will be seen that, if the light strikes the air/glass interface at right angles to (normal to) the interface, it travels on without change of direction, as at *a*. If, however, the light meets the interface at an angle, as at *b*, it is bent or deviated away from the normal on emerging into the air. At increasing angles, e.g. *c*, the deviation becomes greater until the light emerges at almost glancing incidence along the interface. If the angle be increased further, as at *d*, the light will no longer emerge but will be totally reflected back into the glass. This happens whenever light passes from a denser medium (in this case, glass) into a rarer one (air), and the angle at which total internal reflection occurs is called the *critical angle*.

If we regard the glass in the above example as the cover-glass over a microscope specimen, it will be seen that, provided that the angle of the light in the glass is below the critical angle, it will emerge into the air and can then be admitted through the front lens into an objective. There are cases, however, where we require light of greater angle than the critical angle in order to fill the front lens of an objective, which is the case when we use objectives of the highest powers. If air is present, obviously none of these wide angle rays will emerge. But, if the air is replaced by some medium, say oil, of the same optical density (*refractive index*) as that of glass, no deviation or internal reflection takes place when the light emerges

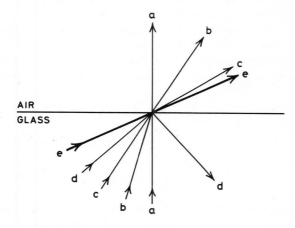

Fig. 7. Critical angle

from the glass and the light travels on in a straight line, see *e*. If we now immerse the front lens of the objective in this oil which has replaced the air, the light will continue to travel into the front lens without deviation.

The oil just mentioned is a special oil whose refractive index has been adjusted to match that of the glass to which it is applied, and is known as Immersion Oil. Objectives which require immersion oil are the 3·6 mm and the 2 mm.

A few special water-immersion objectives are made for use in cases where the specimen has to be immersed in water and a high-powered objective requiring wide angles of light, has to be employed. In these cases both the specimen and the front lens of the objective are immersed in the water, and the objectives are specially marked Water-Immersion.

Resolution

It is stated at the beginning of this chapter that the function of an objective is not only to provide magnification, but, in addition, to elicit the fine detail in various structures. This ability to show fine detail, distinct from its surroundings, is termed *resolution*, which may be defined as the ability of an objective to show small adjacent details as separate entities.

Let us suppose that a certain structure contains two small dots, very close to each other. It might be possible with a given objective after careful focusing to produce a shape like *a*, which is not a true representation of the two dots. With another objective, of the same magnification, we might achieve the result as at *b*, which, again, is not quite a representation of two dots. With a third objective, still of the same magnification, we could achieve the result shown at *c*.

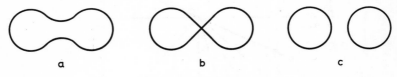

a   b   c

Fig. 8. Resolution

Note that in this latter case the *separation* between the dots is now visible. When such separation has become visible we say that the objective has *resolved* the two dots, and the ability to do so is spoken of as the *resolving power* of the objective. It might be noted, for interest, that objectives of the highest possible resolving power, used under optimum conditions, are just capable of resolving a separation of 0·25 micron ($0·25 \times 10^{-4}$ cm), and this represents the *limit of resolution* of the optical microscope. In Fig. 8 it is assumed that the space between the dots is not less than 0·25 μ, as, otherwise, the dots would appear to overlap.

Numerical Aperture

A certain amount of resolving power is built into every objective, and it is measured and described in terms of the numerical aperture (N.A.) of the objective. From Fig. 9, it will be seen that from every point of the object light emerges in all directions, and that there will be a certain sized cone of light which can just enter the front lens of an objective focused on to the object. Let us call the size of this cone $\angle y$. Take half of angle *y*, known as the *angle of aperture*, and call it x. The medium through which the objective is working—air, oil or water—has a certain refractive index, N. Then $\sin x \times N =$ N.A. (numerical aperture).

This N.A. is just a number for comparison purposes and it indicates the resolving power of the objective. As it is associated with

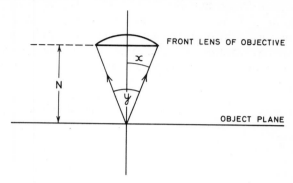

Fig. 9. Angle of aperture and N.A.

the size of the angle of aperture which, in turn, varies with the working distance of the objective (see Table, p. 22), it will be seen that as the power of the objective increases, the working distance decreases, and the angle of aperture increases. Also, as resolving power depends on the size of the angle of aperture, the numerical aperture increases with the higher powered objectives.

Various features are associated with and controlled by numerical aperture:

1. Resolution. An increase in the N.A. means an increase in resolution, or, in other words, resolution varies directly as the N.A.

2. Light transmission. The amount of light passed through an object varies directly as the N.A.

3. Working distance. As the N.A. increases, the working distance is shortened—or, working distance varies inversely as the N.A.

4. Flatness of field. It will be noticed that certain objectives, when focused so that the centre of the field is sharp, show a falling off of sharpness towards the margin of the field, as though the specimen were curved instead of flat. The flatness is controlled by N.A. and it varies inversely with the N.A.—greater N.A. means a reduction of flatness.

5. Depth of field. Sometimes called depth of focus, is controlled by the N.A. and it, too, varies inversely with the N.A.

From the foregoing it will be seen that the N.A. of an objective is at least as important as the magnification. High N.A.'s involve additional lens elements in an objective and, hence, extra cost. Taking prices ruling at the time of writing, an objective of 2 mm focal length with N.A. 1·30 costs £14, while another objective of the same focal length but with N.A. 1·37 costs £44. Note that the difference in N.A. is only 0·07, and yet this produces the huge increase in price. Obviously the more expensive objective must have more advanced features, particularly in the resolving power.

Various features of some common objectives are shown in the following table.

Focal Length	Magnification	Working Distance	N.A.
40 mm ($1\frac{1}{2}$ in.)	× 4	18 mm	0·13
16 mm ($\frac{2}{3}$ in.)	× 10	7 mm	0·28
4 mm ($\frac{1}{6}$ in.)	× 40	1 mm	0·70
3·6 mm ($\frac{1}{7}$ in.)	× 45	0·7 mm	0·94
2 mm ($\frac{1}{12}$ in.)	× 100	0·12 mm	1·30

Flat Field Objectives

Until fairly recently, it was accepted that flat fields were incompatible with high numerical apertures, and this was a source of trouble particularly in photomicrography.

Most makers can now offer objectives with flat fields, particularly the 4 mm, in which there has been no serious loss of resolution due to a reduction of the apertures. This has been achieved by making the objectives more complex by the addition of extra lens elements and, while the fields have been flattened, the cost, inevitably, has been increased. If, therefore, flatness of field is really necessary it is now available, at a price.

Spherical Aberration

Simple lenses are subject to certain defects which prevent the formation of clear images, especially with lenses of medium and high powers.

Consider Fig. 10. Here we have a single lens and, on the axis, an object, say a point O, which emits light. Rays of light travel out in all directions and some of them enter the lens. As they pass through the lens they are bent, and are then bent further as they emerge. Finally the emerging rays come to a meeting point on the axis where an image of the original object is formed.

If we examine the rays which pass through the lens near the centre, we see that they come to a focus at, say, A where they form an image of the object whereas other rays passing through the lens nearer to the margin are bent to a greater degree and come to a focus at a point nearer to the lens than A, say at B, forming

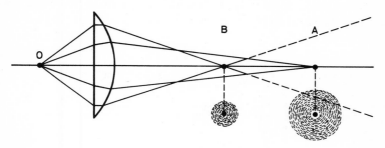

Fig. 10. Spherical aberration

another image there. Depending on where the rays pass through the lens, images are produced at various distances along the axis.

If we examine the image produced at, say, B we see not only the image of the object but a penumbra or halo of unfocused light which makes the image blurred and without sharp outline. Similarly at A we have another image but again surrounded by unfocused light. In this case, rays which have already met on the axis and then diverged again, prevent the sharp definition of the image. In neither case have we a true image of the original object.

In other words, it is not possible to form true and clear images of anything when using a single lens, and the thicker the lens (and, hence, the more powerful the lens) the worse is this defect, which is called *spherical aberration*.

Chromatic Aberration

The diagram of a single lens and its axis has been drawn again, and the object O is a point of white light (Fig. 11). White light is a mixture of all the colours of the spectrum. The rays of light are emitted in all directions from the object and some of them enter the lens where, as before, they are bent in passing through and again on emerging. But the amount of bending depends upon the colour (or wave-length) of the light. It can be shown that light of long wave-length (red light) is bent least of all, while shorter wave-lengths (yellow, green, blue, etc.) are bent progressively more and more, until the shortest wave-length (violet) undergoes the most bending. When the rays are bent, they eventually meet on the axis of the lens where they form an image but the image is in the colour of the meeting rays. Thus we get a series of images in each of the colours, at varying distances from the lens—red, furthest away, followed by orange, yellow, green, blue, indigo and finally violet nearest to the lens, as indicated in the diagram (Fig. 11).

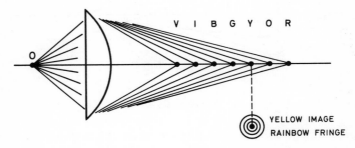

Fig. 11. Chromatic aberration

If we examine any one of these images, say the yellow one, we find that not only is the yellow image an untrue reproduction of the original *white* point, but that it is not clear and sharp as it is surrounded by a halo of unfocused light of other colours, producing a rainbow-like fringe.

As before, it is not possible to produce true and clear images of anything which is emitting light of more than one colour, and again, as before, the thicker the lens the greater is this defect, which is called *chromatic aberration*.

Both of these defects exist simultaneously in any single lens, and are increased in thicker lenses. Thus it was not possible to make optical instruments of high power, which require thick lenses, until the remedy for these defects was found.

Achromatic Lenses

The remedy for both spherical and chromatic aberration was found by an optical worker named Amici about 1810.

Suppose that, for a certain purpose, a thick lens is required.

From what has been said, it will be understood that such a lens is incapable of producing clear images due to its spherical and chromatic aberrations. But if the lens be made in two parts, as indicated in Fig. 12, a convex part and a concave part cemented together, and one element be made of crown glass and the other of flint glass of suitable proportions, then the errors of both spherical and chromatic aberration introduced by the convex lens are cancelled out by equal, but opposite errors introduced by the concave lens.

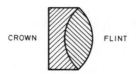

CROWN   FLINT

Fig. 12. Achromatic doublet lens

This means that, whereas the marginal rays of the convex lens focus nearer to the lens that the central rays, the central rays of the concave lens will focus nearer than the marginal rays, and, similarly, for the various colours: for as the aberrations exist simultaneously, their correction can be carried out simultaneously.

With the two aberrations cancelled out, it becomes possible to use thick lenses of high power, and, hence, to make optical instruments of higher magnification. Such a compound lens is termed a *doublet*, and it is known as an *achromatic* lens. This name is derived from "a", meaning "without", and "chromatic" referring to chromatic aberration. And, as the two aberrations are corrected simultaneously, the name indicates, by inference, the correction of the spherical aberration.

Types of Objectives

As the microscope has to be used for such a wide range of purposes, there are several types of objectives available, each calculated to produce the best results for a particular purpose.

Achromatic. As the name implies, these objectives contain at least one achromatic doublet, and, in most cases, more than one, and they represent the minimum of correction necessary for microscopy. They are of moderate numerical aperture, hence of moderate resolving power; they have a reasonably long working distance and a reasonably flat field of view. They are the maids-of-all-work for the microscope and are widely used in student microscopes where the structures to be examined do not call for the maximum possible resolution at any particular magnification. They are the objectives used in most routine microscopes in hospital and industrial laboratories. They are easy to use in that they do not call for ultra-precise setting-up, and, being less complex than other types, are the least expensive.

Apochromatic. In describing the achromatic lens, it was stated that a doublet lens of suitable materials and proportions would correct the basic aberrations. This is not strictly true, for such a simple doublet, while correcting the major errors, does not do so perfectly, and there are still residual errors which would prevent the making of objectives of the highest aperture and performance. The complexity of the lenses has to be increased to carry out these corrections to a greater degree, and, in place of the doublet, lenses are made as triplets, see Fig. 13, and in place of the elementary crown and flint glasses, many kinds of special glass, and even

Fig. 13. Apochromatic triplet lens

of materials which are not glass, are employed. Combinations of doublets, triplets and specially shaped single lenses are made to produce the *apochromatic* objective. By derivation, the prefix "apo", from the Greek, indicates "away from" or "detached", and "chromatic" refers to the chromatic aberration. These objectives are made to give perfect colour rendering; they have very high numerical apertures—hence, very high resolution and all else associated with high aperture—and they are expensive. In the visual microscope, these objectives, suitably fed with well controlled light, give the highest possible performance, and they are, therefore, used in research work where high resolution is required, and in other work where the material being examined, such as particles of finely divided substances, is of size near to the limit of resolution. Further, owing to the perfection of their colour correction, they are frequently preferred for colour photomicrography.

The following objectives are made in the apochromatic series:

Focal Length	Magnification	N.A.
16 mm	× 9	0·30
8 mm	× 20	0·65
4 mm	× 40	0·85
2 mm	× 90	1·37

Fluorite. Intermediate between achromatic and apochromatic objectives but nearer to the latter, there is a type known as the fluorite objective. As has been said in connection with apochromatic objectives, materials other than glass, which can be ground and polished, are used in lens making. One such material is fluorite, a natural mineral, which gives the name to this type of objective. It must not be assumed that all the lenses of a fluorite objective are made of this mineral, but more of it is employed than in other objectives. One of the characteristics of a fluorite objective is the increase in contrast between parts of an object and their surroundings, such contrast often assisting in the seeing, and also the photographic recording of fine detail.

Also, because fluorite does not render all colours perfectly, this property is made use of in certain work in some hospital laboratories. A film of Tubercle Bacillus in sputum is generally stained by the Ziehl–Neelson staining process which produces pale pink organisms on a pale blue background. When there are very few organisms present, the lack of contrast between them and their background makes searching for them both laborious and frequently erratic as they can be easily missed. Using a fluorite objective, the pale pink of the organism is translated into a deep magenta shade making even single organisms stand out prominently against the background and making examination of the film both easy and more accurate.

Because the numerical apertures of fluorite objectives are high, their employment is affected by the limitations imposed by high aperture. Usually only two powers of fluorite objectives are made:

Focal Length	Magnification	N.A.
3·6 mm	× 50	0·95
2 mm	× 90	1·30

Both are oil-immersion objectives, but sometimes there is added to the series a 16 mm, × 10, N.A. 0·30, objective which is a partial fluorite objective designed to work in this series.

Uncovered Objects

The presence or absence of a cover-glass does not really affect the working of either low-power objectives of focal length 16 mm or lower, or of oil-immersion types. But the 4 mm is very sensitive and most makers offer the 4 mm in two forms—corrected for use through a cover-glass, or corrected for uncovered objects. Used incorrectly, the 4 mm cannot produce clear images, the whole field being covered by a milky haze which cannot be cleared by focusing or by diaphragm control of the condenser.

CHAPTER 3

The Eyepiece

The second basic optical unit of the microscope is the eyepiece. As has already been discussed, the objective supplies the initial magnified image which contains all the available detail which that particular objective can provide, but the magnification is comparatively low, the maximum being × 100.

The prime purpose of the eyepiece is to magnify the image produced by the objective, and to present this magnified image to the eye. The combination of primary magnification, due to the objective, and eyepiece magnification gives the *total magnification* of the microscope.

Types of Eyepieces

All eyepieces have a common purpose, that of magnification, and the amount of magnification is engraved on the top of the eyepiece. The powers currently available are × 4, × 5, × 6, × 8, × 10, × 15 and × 20. But, as there are different types of objectives for certain purposes, so there are various types of eyepieces which have purposes additional to magnification, to match the requirements of the objectives.

Huyghenian. This eyepiece, sometimes called Huyghens, is the one associated with all achromatic objectives, and its purpose is for magnification only. It consists of two plano-convex lenses, mounted with the convex faces towards the objective, with a metal diaphragm in between them, located at the focal plane of the top or eye-lens. The bottom lens, the field-lens, collects the rays of light coming up the microscope from the objective and brings them to a focus in the plane of the diaphragm. As this latter is in the focal plane of the eye-lens, the image is visible through the eye-lens which provides the magnification of the eyepiece.

Pointer Eyepieces. One variant of the Huyghenian eyepiece is provided with an adjustable pointer which can be set to indicate some minute detail of interest in the field of view. It is used mainly in teaching to ensure that various observers are looking at the same detail if they use the microscope in succession.

Compensating Eyepieces. From what has been said about the colour correction in objectives, it might be thought that no colour errors existed after the light had gone through the objective. This is not quite correct, and there are cases where some residual colour error is deliberately left for final correction by the eyepiece. These compensating eyepieces have, in addition to their magnification, a lens arrangement designed to add the final correction of chromatic aberration, and they are of great assistance in perfecting the images from apochromatic and fluorite objectives and, also, from achromatic objectives of the higher powers.

In some cases, the compensating eyepiece is used to correct excessive curvature of field which is associated with objectives of high numerical aperture.

Holoscopic Eyepieces (Watson). These are special eyepieces of the colour compensating type but made with a short draw-tube carrying the eye-lens. Adjustment of the tube alters the degree of compensation, and these eyepieces can, therefore, be used on a wide range of objectives, from achromats to apochromats, and thereby the need to provide various eyepieces to match individual objectives is avoided.

Telaugic (Swift), *Periplanatic* (Leitz), *Homal* (Zeiss), *Planoscopic* (Spencer) are names given by various manufacturers to eyepieces designed to reduce curvature of field, and they are all, essentially, of the same type. The Telaugic, in addition, offers a very wide field and is sometimes called a wide-angle eyepiece.

Complec (Watson). Most spectacle wearers cannot get their eye close enough to the eye-lens to see a full field of view. As a result, they have to move their spectacle lens over the eyepiece and explore the field gradually. This is an inconvenience and, further, the movement of the spectacle lens over the eye-lens can scratch one or both of the lenses in the most critical part through which normal observation is made.

The Complec eyepiece is of the compensating type, but of special design with a large eye-lens, a raised eye-point and a rubber guard over the rim of the eyepiece. A spectacle wearer can safely rest his lens against the rubber guard and then see the whole of the field of view without moving his head.

Ramsden and Kellner. These eyepieces, which are very similar to each other, differ from all the preceding ones in that the plane of focus of the eye-lens lies just below the field-lens, external to the eyepiece. The field-lens is a plano-convex lens with the convex face away from the objective. Having the plane of focus below the eye-piece allows the easy positioning of graticules, traversing hair-lines, and so on, and these types are generally used in some applications in micrometry (see Chapter 7).

Special Eyepieces. These have been developed for various uses in micrometry and are listed here for a record of their names: Micrometer, Screw Micrometer, Ehrlich, and Image Shearing. In Chapter 7 they are discussed in detail.

Projection Eyepieces. A few eyepieces are made under this name. They are of the Huyghenian type but with an achromatic eye-lens mounted in an adjustable sleeve. The eye-lens has a cap with a very small hole located at the plane of focus of the emerging cone of light and it is designed to reduce stray light. By sliding the eye-lens in or out of the eyepiece, a sharp image of the diaphragm within the eyepiece can be projected on to the film or plate in photomicrography, even when the camera has an extensible bellows. The aperture in the diaphragm is smaller than usual, thus cutting off some of the marginal part of the field which is often out of focus when the centre is sharp. The result of this is to make the photograph appear flat all over.

Parfocal Eyepieces. Because eyepieces of different powers are of different lengths, refocusing of the objective would be required for each change of eyepiece. Most makers now fit to the eyepieces tubular collars of varying lengths so arranged that if the objective is focused for any one eyepiece, other eyepieces can be introduced without the need for refocusing. The eyepieces are then said to be parfocal, and the collars used are called parfocalling collars.

Selection of Eyepiece Power

Total magnification must be kept within certain limits, defined as not exceeding $\times 1000$. N.A. for achromatic objectives, or $\times 1500$. N.A. for fluorites and apochromatics. Within these limits there can be cases where the same total magnification can be obtained by several combinations of objective and eyepiece. For example, $\times 200$ total can be obtained from objective $\times 10$ with eyepiece $\times 20$, from objective $\times 20$ with eyepiece $\times 10$ or from objective $\times 40$ with eyepiece $\times 5$. Which combination should be used?

Regarding the objectives first of all, the higher the power, the greater is the N.A., and, therefore, the greater is the resolution. So, if resolution be the main purpose in using this magnification, the × 40 objective would be the choice. However, if depth of focus and size of field of view can be of some importance, some resolution will have to be sacrificed by using a lower power of objective which has greater depth and coverage of the specimen.

As for the eyepieces, the higher the power, the more difficult is the eyepiece to use, and any small blemishes such as dust particles, become more visible and troublesome. Further, as the eyepiece power increases, the size of field diminishes. For interest, it may be recorded that, of all the available powers of eyepieces, the × 6 has the largest field of all, even larger than × 5 or × 4.

The general rule can, therefore, be given that consistent with obtaining sufficient resolution, depth and field for a given purpose, the highest power of objective used with the lowest power of eyepiece is to be preferred.

CHAPTER 4

The Condenser

The third basic optical unit of the microscope is the condenser, which might rightly be termed the Cinderella of the microscope in that it is so often abused, misused or even forgotten. As will be shown, the performance of an expensive, well-corrected objective can largely be spoiled by using it with an incorrect condenser or even with a suitable condenser incorrectly adjusted.

The prime purpose of all condensers is to illuminate the object at the point on which the objective is focused, and to fill the field of view with uniform illumination. Most users are aware of this, but it is frequently forgotten that the condenser has a second and very important purpose—to supply the objective with a cone of light of the right size and character to enable it to produce its maximum

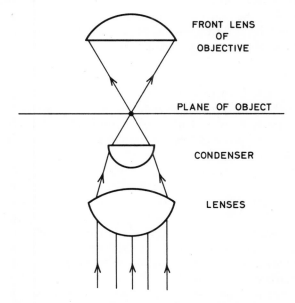

Fig. 14. Light from condenser to objective

result. It will be remembered that, to produce the maximum resolution and associated features, the front lens of an objective must receive from every point on the object a cone of light of sufficient size to fill the front lens, as shown in Fig. 14. But a moment's thought will show that such a cone must originate from somewhere below the object—in fact, from the lens system of the condenser. Further, as the objective demands a solid cone of light, i.e. one in which all rays originate from the same point in the object, the condenser must supply a cone of similar nature in which all rays central, marginal and of all wave-lengths or colours, are focused at one point on the object. Unless the condenser can do this, the objective cannot receive a solid cone of the size demanded and the effective N.A. of the objective is thereby reduced.

Types of Condensers

As there are varieties of objective types for different purposes, and numbers of different powers of objectives within these types, it cannot be expected that any one condenser can supply the requirements of every objective. Nor can the alternative, of having a series of matching condensers for a range of objectives, ideal as this may be, be entertained, on the grounds of cost and slowness of working. This results in the condenser having, in most cases, to be a compromise so that the best possible results may be obtained within the limits of one, or at most, two condensers.

Simple Abbe

This type has been used for a long time, but it was popularized by the work of Ernst Abbe around 1875. It consists of two large diameter plano-convex lenses of considerable thickness, air-separated, with an adjustable iris diaphragm mounted at the back focal plane.

From what has been said about spherical and chromatic aberrations, it will be realized that such a lens system is incapable of focusing light entering it into a solid cone in which all rays, central, marginal and of different wave-lengths will meet at a point on the object. Optically speaking, this is a most inefficient optical unit, and it cannot do more than illuminate the object. In fact, some workers deny it the right to the name of "condenser" and speak of it as the "Abbe Illuminator".

Because of its inherent errors, the Abbe is insensitive to critical focusing or accurate centring and, therefore, in student and other inexpert hands, no great harm to the performance of the objective can result from maladjustment of the condenser. Furthermore, because of its simple construction, it is inexpensive. As one might expect, for these reasons the Abbe is to be found on practically all student microscopes and on many of the simpler routine microscopes where a high degree of performance is not expected or necessary. In use, the iris diaphragm comes into play and the reader is referred to the section on Condenser Apertures below.

Three-Lens Abbe

In an attempt to reduce the gross errors of the simple Abbe, some makers offer the three-lens Abbe, which, as its name implies, consists of three plano-convex lenses. But, as these are thick lenses, air-separated, the chromatic and spherical aberrations are still very pronounced. Only if this condenser is used with monochromatic light is there any real improvement over the simple Abbe.

Achromatic and Aplanatic

These two names are practically interchangeable, indicating, as they do, the correction of chromatic and spherical aberrations respectively. As the errors are co-existent, they are corrected simultaneously.

This type of condenser is constructed very much on the lines of the objective itself, having multiple lenses including, sometimes, two doublets or even a triplet lens, as shown in Fig. 15. Resulting

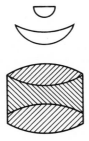

Fig. 15. Corrected condenser

from the complex lens systems and the elimination of the major part of the two aberrations, the condenser is able to focus all the light in one plane and in the field of an objective, thereby producing the solid cone of light which the objective demands. Because of this critical focal point, this type of condenser, to perform at its best, requires that the object be mounted on a glass slide whose thickness does not exceed some maximum figure. Most manufacturers make this condenser to work through slides up to a maximum thickness of 1·5 mm.

A further result of the critical focus point of this condenser is the need for careful focusing (as discussed in Chapter 5) and for accurate centring to ensure that the optical centres of condenser and objective are on the same axis.

Oil-Immersion

When describing objectives the point was made that, to utilize very wide angles of light as required by high N.A., all air between the object and the objective had to be eliminated by the substitution of immersion oil for the air, and so prevent total internal reflection of light in the cover-glass at angles beyond the critical angle. In the same way, as it is required that light of very high angle must emerge from the condenser and enter the glass slide on its way to the objective, all air between the top of the condenser and the underside of the slide must be replaced by immersion oil, and there are special condensers made, in construction similar to oil-immersion objectives, to work under this condition of oil-immersion. These are discussed further under condenser apertures. The remarks about focusing and centring in achromatic and aplanatic condensers apply with even more force to these oil-immersion condensers.

Special Condensers

The following special condensers are described in the appropriate chapters, shown in brackets: Macro (Photomicrography); Dark-Ground (Dark-Ground Illumination); Trilux (Phase-Contrast); Heine (Phase-Contrast); Auxiliary (Köhler Illumination, Chapter 5).

Condenser Apertures

In the chapter on objectives, considerable mention of numerical aperture has been made, and from Fig. 14 it will be seen that the full N.A. of the objective can be achieved only if the condenser is supplying a solid cone of light of similar aperture. This solid cone from the condenser is termed the *Aplanatic Aperture* of the condenser and it indicates the size of cone which is free from spherical aberration, i.e. in which both the central and marginal rays are focused in the same plane.

The *effective aperture* of any objective–condenser combination is the mean of the N.A. of the objective and the aplanatic aperture of the condenser. It is important to distinguish between this aplanatic aperture and the *total aperture* of the condenser, and misleading statements are sometimes met in catalogues and other literature.

For example, catalogues have been published which list the simple Abbe condenser with N.A. 1·40. Whilst this may be impressive to the uninitiated it is obviously very misleading. In the first place, no condenser however perfect its corrections can possibly have a total aperture greater than N.A. 1·0 if it has to work through air. Only by substituting immersion oil for the air can the aperture exceed N.A. 1·0. Then, unless the condenser has been properly calculated to work through oil, no increase in effective aperture or in light transmission is obtained by oil immersion. But, above all, while an Abbe condenser may have a large total aperture, it is so full of basic aberrations that the light which it is unable to focus in one plane produces only *glare* which, in fact, detracts from the performance of the objective.

To eliminate glare, use has to be made of the iris diaphragm of the condenser to cut off all the marginal rays so that the central rays only are used. Doing this reduces the glare, but also reduces the aperture of the condenser, and in the case of the Abbe, the aperture which is aplanatic is the very much reduced one of about N.A. 0·45 —very different from the total aperture as advertised!

To illustrate the result of combining N.A. of the objective with aplanatic aperture of the condenser, consider the following case, which is by no means unusual or extreme:

(a) Objective N.A. 1·30. Abbe condenser, aplanatic aperture 0·45.

$$\text{Effective aperture} = \frac{1\cdot30 + 0\cdot45}{2} = \frac{1\cdot75}{2} = 0\cdot875$$

(b) Objective N.A. 1·30. Achromatic condenser, aplanatic aperture 0·95.

$$\text{Effective aperture} = \frac{1\cdot30 + 0\cdot95}{2} = \frac{2\cdot25}{2} = 1\cdot125$$

(c) Objective N.A. 1·30. Oil-immersion condenser, aplanatic aperture 1·30.

$$\text{Effective aperture} = \frac{1\cdot30 + 1\cdot30}{2} = \frac{2\cdot60}{2} = 1\cdot30$$

In combination (a), the efficiency of a 2 mm oil-immersion objective has been reduced to little more than that of a good quality 4 mm objective. In combination (b), this same objective is performing sufficiently well for most purposes, but it has lost some of its efficiency. In combination (c), as the aperture of the condenser matches that of the objective, we have the ideal condition, and the N.A. of the objective can be used to its maximum efficiency.

It should be noted that the condenser used in (c) in oil-immersion is designed so that it can be used dry, also. In this event, the aplanatic aperture of the condenser is reduced to N.A. 0·95, so that conditions would then be very similar to combination (b).

Condenser Apertures

Type	Total Aperture		Aplanatic Aperture	
	Dry	Immersed	Dry	Immersed
Abbe	1·0	1·25	0·45	—
Achromatic	1·0	—	0·95	—
less top lens	0·50	—	0·40	—
Immersion	—	1·30	—	1·30
used dry	1·0	—	0·90	—
less top lens	0·60	—	0·55	—

Field Coverage

When a condenser is properly focused, it should produce an image of the light source on the object at the point where the objective is focused. The higher the power of the condenser the more the light is condensed onto a very small area of the object, and the brightness is thereby at its maximum. This is the ideal condition of use.

It can happen, however, that a high power condenser, properly focused, will produce an image of the light source too small to fill the field of view. The theoretically perfect way of dealing with this situation is to substitute a condenser of lower power which will produce an image of larger size of the light source, big enough to fill the field. Failing this, as it is usually impracticable, most condensers are made with a removable top lens, which, on removal, leaves the correcting lenses to deal with the aberrations and changes the condenser to a lower power (i.e. with longer focal length and smaller aperture) usually enough to provide full field coverage with the condenser properly focused.

But there are many cases, in histology for example, where preliminary searching of the material is done through the 40 mm "scanner" objective followed by the 16 mm and finally by the 4 mm. If the condenser power is lowered sufficiently to fill the field of the 40 mm and 16 mm objectives, the 4 mm will be starved of aperture and cannot then yield its full resolution, light-transmission, etc.

Under these circumstances a compromise must be made to allow the histologist to proceed with his work with the minimum of interruption and delay. There are three possible ways of doing this: (a) A lightly ground glass disc, to act as a diffuser, is placed in the swing-out filter carrier below the condenser. With the diffuser in position on the axis, uniform illumination of the full field is obtained even for the low power objectives, while, on reaching the high power, the diffuser having been swung out of the axis, the full condenser remains to feed the requirements of the top power objective.

(b) Despite what has been said against the use of the concave mirror with a substage condenser, a permissible departure from perfection can be made in cases like this. The concave mirror working with the condenser gives a sufficiently even illumination to cover the field of the low power objectives and while the condenser cannot now yield the correct cone of light required for the 4 mm objective, the result is sufficiently good for much general routine work. It must be understood, however, that in cases where the full resolution of the 4 mm is necessary to confirm a diagnosis, this combination is usually inadequate, and resource must be made to conventional microscopy as outlined earlier in this section.

(c) A further method of dealing with this problem lies in the use of a condenser fitted with a top lens which can be swung out of the axis by a lever. This removal of the top lens leaves a low power condenser which serves to fill the low power objectives, while a flick of the lever will restore the high power condenser for the high power objective.

Important

Under no circumstances should the user be allowed to effect a compromise by lowering the condenser below its correct focal distance. This is wrong, optically, and can lead to spurious results,

4

artifacts, etc., and with the three techniques (a), (b) and (c) above, being available, it should never be necessary.

It may be asked, how can a condenser which produces an aplanatic cone of greater aperture than the N.A. of the objective be used satisfactorily. If the condenser is used at full aperture, the unwanted aperture produces glare, to the detraction of image quality, without contributing anything to image formation.

It is for cases like this that the iris diaphragm is provided. By closing the diaphragm the size of the aplanatic cone of the condenser is reduced until it matches the requirement of the objective, thereby eliminating all glare, while retaining sufficient aperture for the objective. There is, therefore, a specific size of diaphragm opening for every objective with which the condenser is used, and the adjusting of this size is of considerable importance in the correct functioning of the microscope. Methods for obtaining this result are described in Chapter 5.

CHAPTER 5

Using the Microscope

Setting-up procedures are of the greatest importance and should be mastered by every user of a microscope, so that the maximum potential of every lens is obtained. The procedure should be in definite steps, followed in sequence, and these steps are now discussed in relation to the three most usual combinations of microscope and illuminant, viz.:

A. Student microscope with bench lamp
B. Student microscope with built-in lamp
C. Advanced microscope with Köhler illumination.

Where there is any choice as to the position in a room where microscopy is to be done, always choose a bench or table where the user has his back to a window or strong room light, with as much shade over the microscope as can be contrived. Such an arrangement eliminates much glare from the bench and from the window, reducing fatigue in the eyes, and promoting much better contrast in the object and the easier observation of fine detail. The worst possible site for microscopy is on a bench in front of a large window without any blind or shade and facing the sun, and, although it would seem to be so obvious, such a bad position can often be seen in many laboratories.

A. Student Microscope with Bench Lamp

1. Examine the microscope. Identify the objectives, and the control lever of the substage iris diaphragm. If there is a draw-tube, set the tube-length to the distance prescribed by the maker.
2. Place the lamp about 10 in. from the microscope, and direct the plain mirror towards the lamp.
3. Raise the substage until the top of the condenser is level with the stage. Open the iris diaphragm fully.
4. Place a specimen on the stage. Select a ×5 or ×6 eyepiece and insert in the eyepiece tube, and rotate the nosepiece to bring the lowest powered objective into the axis, above the condenser.

5. With the eye at the side of the eyepiece, look at the top of the condenser and adjust the mirror position until this top lens of the condenser appears to be full of light.

6. With the objective raised to more than its working distance, apply the eye to the eyepiece, and, using the coarse adjustment only, lower the objective until the specimen begins to come into view. If the specimen is coloured, the colour will appear before any detail can be seen. Continue to lower the objective slowly, still using coarse adjustment only until the specimen is sharply focused. (*Note.* It is a mark of a competent microscopist to be able to focus a 16 mm objective by the coarse adjustment only. Use of the fine adjustment is, in any case, a waste of time with this low power of objective, as the adjustment is so slow.)

It is probable that the field of view is not evenly illuminated. If so, tilt the mirror slightly until the whole field is evenly illuminated and the illumination is of the highest possible intensity.

7. The condenser must now be focused. If the lamp is provided with a diaphragm, close this and focus the substage condenser up or down until a clear image of the diaphragm is seen superimposed on the specimen. It can be made clearer if the substage diaphragm be partially closed. The lamp diaphragm is then opened to just clear the field of view. Should the field be not fully covered with the diaphragm at full aperture, then, either the top lens of the substage condenser must be removed, and refocusing of this condenser repeated, or a diffuser must be introduced into the filter carrier below the condenser.

If the lamp has no diaphragm, hold a rod or pencil against the lamp bulb at its brightest part, and focus the substage condenser to produce an image of the rod or pencil superimposed on the specimen, again using the partially closed substage diaphragm for the clearest image.

8. Aperture adjustment. It has already been stressed that the size of the cone of light produced by the substage condenser must match the numerical aperture of the objective. There are two methods whereby this can be done.

(a) This method appears in most textbooks on microscopy. After completing step 7, the eyepiece should be removed from the microscope. By looking down into the body, an illuminated disc can be seen at the bottom, in fact, the back lens of the objective. If the lever operating the substage diaphragm is now moved to open and close this diaphragm, it will be seen that as the aperture is closed, an image of the diaphragm can be seen cutting into the back lens from the periphery. The smaller the aperture in the diaphragm, the more the back lens of the objective appears to be blacked-out. The ideal setting for any objective is obtained when $\frac{2}{3}$ or $\frac{3}{4}$ of the back lens appears to be full of light with the outer portion blacked-out. The eyepiece is then replaced and a final touch given to the focusing of the objective should present the best possible image.

(b) The above method involves an interruption to the observation of the specimen and the alternative is, therefore, frequently preferred. During step 7 the eye is at the eyepiece and as soon as the substage condenser is judged to be in focus, the substage diaphragm is opened and closed by the operating lever, and the result observed on the specimen. It will be seen that at full aperture the field of view is flooded with light and frequently looks hazy—this is glare. At the other extreme, the field becomes very dark and outlines are thickened—dots become discs, and so on. The aperture is increased and decreased in shortening strokes until the position is found where the field is just beginning to darken—the so-called Threshold of Darkening. This is the correct aperture for the objective in use, and with very little experience, it can be determined very exactly. As before, a slight refocusing of the objective should present the best possible image.

For interest, the two methods can be compared, for, if at the conclusion of method (b) the eyepiece be removed, and the back lens of the objective inspected, it will be seen that the required $\frac{2}{3}$ to $\frac{3}{4}$ filling of the back lens has been achieved, and with less trouble.

9. It is usual to proceed now to the objective of the next higher power, say the 4 mm. If the objectives are correctly parfocalled, rotation of the nosepiece to bring the 4 mm over the condenser should result in the specimen being seen through the eyepiece almost in focus, and a small movement of the fine adjustment should complete the focusing. But, as this new objective has a higher numerical aperture than the previous one, a re-adjustment of the aperture of the substage condenser must be made, to provide a cone of larger size. Proceed, therefore, by repeating step 8 either (a) or (b), as preferred, and, as before, make a final focusing by the fine adjustment.

10. Some work now calls for the top power objective, say the 2 mm. As this is an oil-immersion type, the procedure is different. First of all, raise the body of the microscope until the last used objective is about 25 mm above the specimen. Rotate the nosepiece

to bring the 2 mm above the condenser. Apply a drop of immersion oil to the top of the specimen immediately above the centre of the condenser. This drop ought to be sufficient to leave an upstanding dome of oil.

Look at the microscope across the stage with the eye level with the stage, and observe the dome of oil. Then, using the coarse adjustment lower the objective until it makes contact with the oil, as indicated by a sudden splash of light from the point of contact. Then, according to the type of objective, proceed as follows:

(a) If the objective is spring-loaded, continue to lower the front into the oil by very gentle use of the coarse adjustment, until it can be seen, and, sometimes, felt that the front of the objective has made contact with the specimen—one indication being that the spring-loaded front is just beginning to be compressed into the body of the objective. Apply the eye to the eyepiece and, using the fine adjustment, very slowly raise the objective until the specimen comes into view, and still more slowly until it is in perfect focus, and then repeat step 8 (a) or (b).

(b) If the objective is not spring-loaded, as soon as it has made contact with the oil, apply the eye to the eyepiece, and still using the coarse adjustment, but with the utmost care, continue to lower the objective into the oil until either the colour of the specimen, if it is stained, or some larger detail becomes just barely visible. Stop and transfer to the fine adjustment and continue delicate movement until focusing is complete. Repeat step 8 (a) or (b) as before. Always remember that this objective has a working distance of only 0·12 mm so that, when in focus, the front lens is very close to the specimen.

B. Student Microscope with Built-in Lamp

If the microscope has a lamp built-in to the base of the instrument, setting-up will be a repeat of steps 1, 3, 4 and 6, the latter as far as the focusing of the objective, and omitting the last paragraph.
7. The substage condenser must now be focused. As most built-in lamps in this type of microscope have a lamp condenser with a ground surface to act as a diffuser, it is usually possible to focus the substage condenser until a pattern of the grinding comes into focus superimposed on the specimen. A slight defocusing of the substage is now permissible to remove this pattern which might be objectionable on certain objects, but only enough defocusing to just remove the patterning. If the lamp condenser is a clear lens, or if it is diffi-

cult to see the pattern of grinding, hold a pencil or rod in contact with the top of the lens and focus the substage condenser until the rod or pencil is clearly seen. Some closure of the substage diaphragm will make this image clearer.

Then proceed with steps 8, 9 and 10 as required by the work being done.

C. Advanced Microscope with Köhler Illumination

The wider appreciation of the importance of controlled illumination in the production of perfect images has resulted in increasing numbers of microscopes being fitted with or supplied with lamps which can provide such controlled light and the system most commonly used is termed Köhler illumination.

Köhler Illumination

This is the modern equivalent of what used to be called Critical Illumination, and its importance lies in the fact that an objective used with any less well controlled light fails to develop its full aperture and all that is associated with this.

The requirements for this technique are: a lamp bulb of high intensity but of very small light-emitting area, mounted in a centring mount or in some pre-focus mount to ensure that the centre of the filament is on the optical axis of the lamp; a focusable lamp condenser with a multi-lens system to correct the basic aberrations; and an adjustable iris diaphragm.

Such a lamp is shown in Fig. 16, which includes a light control unit in which the mains voltage is reduced, usually to 6 volts, and which incorporates a rheostat to control the intensity. Some units, as the one in the illustration, have a voltmeter so that there is visible control of the voltage applied to the filament.

(*Important.* With all lamps with a variable intensity control, the control must be set to minimum intensity before the current is switched on, and reduced again to minimum before switching off. This will greatly prolong the life of the bulb by protecting it against initial electrical surge.)

In using a lamp for Köhler illumination the following steps, in this order, are necessary:

1. The lamp condenser must be focused to produce an image of the light source, the filament, at the back focal plane of the substage condenser, i.e. on the diaphragm located there.
2. The substage condenser must be focused to produce an image

of the lamp diaphragm on the specimen at the point where the objective is focused.

3. The aperture of the lamp diaphragm is opened until its image just clears the margins of the field of view.

4. The substage diaphragm is closed in accordance with step 8 (a) or (b) as in the earlier sections.

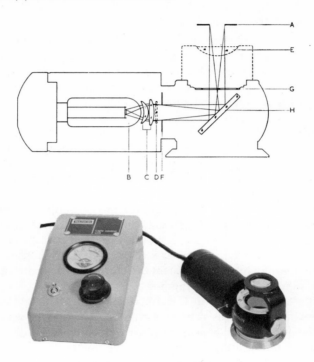

Fig. 16. Köhler illumination lamp

Referring to the diagram in Fig. 16, B is a very concentrated filament pattern, rated at 6 volts, 15 watts; C is the lamp condenser with correcting lenses for aberrations; D is a diffuser; F is the lamp diaphragm; H is a surface-aluminized mirror in a sealed chamber. (Note that a glass mirror here would produce double images of the lamp diaphragm.) G is a transparent cover plate, which can support a colour filter if desired; E indicates an auxiliary lens; A is the diaphragm at the back focal plane of the substage condenser.

In setting up a microscope equipped with such a lamp, the following is the correct sequence: As in section A, above, use steps 1, 3, 4 and 6, omitting the last paragraph of 6. Then:

7. Close the lamp diaphragm and focus the substage condenser to produce a sharp image of this diaphragm superimposed on the specimen. If the image is not perfectly centred to the field, recentre the substage condenser by means of the centring screws provided. Open the lamp diaphragm to just clear the margin of the field.

Repeat 8, 9 and 10, as necessary.

If it happens that when the image of the lamp diaphragm is sharply focused and the full opening of this diaphragm is too small to fill the field, the auxiliary lens can now be introduced, accompanied by the introduction of the diffuser. Under these conditions, full field illumination is obtained even for the lowest powers of objectives, and without any modification or refocusing of the substage condensers.

In all the above cases, certain adjustments can be regarded as basic adjustments in that they are made initially in setting-up but remain unaltered during subsequent work with the microscope. These are, where applicable: the positioning of the lamp and the mirror; the focusing of the lamp condenser; the focusing of the substage condenser (but see below).

There are in addition, other adjustments, which could be termed running adjustments, which have to be altered during the using of the microscope. In general terms it can be made a rule that every change of objective and/or of condenser (and this includes removal and replacement of the top lens) must be accompanied by a checking of centration and by a readjustment of diaphragm apertures.

Centration

Centration is checked as follows:

(a) In microscopes used with lamps without lamp diaphragm, the substage diaphragm is closed and the substage condenser refocused to produce an image of the diaphragm on the specimen. If this is off-centre, the condenser is recentred to the field by the centring screws.

(b) If the lamp has a diaphragm, the substage condenser is refocused, if objective and/or condenser have been changed, to produce an image of the lamp diaphragm on the specimen, and, if necessary, this is centred to the field by the substage centring screws.

Apertures are re-set for a change of objective and/or condenser by repeating steps 7 and 8.

It is not always realized how important is the careful focusing of the substage condenser. This has been demonstrated most strikingly in colour photomicrography. As is well known, errors in focusing a lens in colour work are similar in effect to errors in exposure time, and can produce spurious colours in the finished photograph. It has been shown that even an achromatic condenser, incorrectly focused, can lead to these colour errors and, if a stained biological preparation is photographed in colour, (a) with the condenser carefully focused, (b) with the condenser slightly above focus and (c) with the condenser slightly below focus, three quite different results are obtained. From (a) there is correct colour rendering of the specimen. But from (b) and (c) the whole picture is spoilt by background colour usually reddish-brown, or bluish-green, which does not exist in the specimen. Although for visual work, such colour errors are not easily seen, it will be appreciated that careful focusing of the substage condenser will produce the most perfect image.

Tube Length and Cover-Glass Thickness

Mention has been made of the setting of the tube length to the figure determined by the maker of an objective. This figure is set on the assumption that the thickness of the cover-glass plus mountant is of some predetermined value, usually $0 \cdot 17$–$0 \cdot 18$ mm. Usually with a mounted specimen, this thickness is unknown and unknowable. While low power objectives are insensitive to differences in this thickness, and oil-immersion objectives, because of the homogeneity of the medium between the front lens and the object, are equally unaffected, there are the high powered dry objectives (4 mm and 3 mm) which are particularly sensitive to variations in this thickness, and in *critical microscopy*, certain adjustments must be made when using these objectives. If the adjustment is incorrect there will be a milky haze over the object which cannot be removed by any other means.

There are three ways of making this adjustment:

(a) By varying the tube length by altering the position of the draw-tube.

(b) By using the correcting collar where an objective is so provided.

(c) By using the Jackson Tube-Length Corrector.

The correcting collar is a fitting within the objective whereby rotation of the collar alters the separation between the lens elements in the objective. It has a series of divisions against the rotating collar, marked from 0 (which is the setting for an object without a cover-glass) through figures such as 0·10, 0·15, 0·18, 1·10, 1·15, etc. which represent the thickness of cover-glass plus mountant, in millimetres.

The Jackson Tube-Length Corrector (by Watsons) is a fitting which is mounted between the objective and the body of the microscope. It has a rotating ring, and a scale marked from 100 to 300, which figures represent the effective tube length of the microscope.

Both the correcting collar and the tube-length corrector are particularly valuable for binocular microscopes where there is no other method of making this correction.

In use, there are two methods of observation, which will now be described:

1. Focus the objective, selecting some very small detail approaching a dot in shape and size, and set the substage iris diaphragm about one-quarter open. While observing the detail, open the diaphragm to about three-quarters open and notice if there is any change of focusing required to maintain sharp focus. If the object goes out of focus at different openings of the diaphragm the tube length is incorrect for this particular specimen.

(a) If the draw-tube is used for correction, alter the tube length by, say, 10 mm and repeat the test. Eventually a tube length will be found at which there is no appreciable change of focus at any opening of the diaphragm, and this is the correct tube length for this specimen.

(b) If a correcting collar is used on the objective, do the above test, moving the collar by one division at a time.

(c) If the tube-length corrector is used, follow the same procedure as (b).

2. The second method is more precise, but rather more difficult in use, at least until the operator has become used to this observation. The objective is focused on to some dot in the specimen, with the condenser properly focused and the various apertures correctly set. Using the fine adjustment, the objective is raised and lowered by equal distances above and below the focus point, and the object is observed critically during this time. If the tube length, or the correcting collar, or the tube-length corrector are correctly set for the thickness of cover-glass plus mountant of this particular specimen, it will be seen that the dot becomes a rather hazy disc of grey with

the objective either above or below the point of focus, and that the disc appears the same at either position. If, however, the thickness of cover-glass plus mountant is different from that for which the tube length, etc., have been set, then on one side of focus the dot becomes a hazy grey disc with a dark centre, and at the other side of focus it becomes a dark ring with a light centre.

To make the correction, find the position where the dark ring with light centre is seen, and, without altering the focus of the objective, move the draw-tube, or correcting collar, or tube-length corrector to bring the dot back into focus. After this has been done correctly, and it may require more than one attempt, it should now be found that raising and lowering the objective above and below focus will result in the dot becoming a greyish disc of the same appearance at each side of focus.

It may be surprising to note the amount by which tube length has to be altered for very small differences of cover-glass plus mountant thickness. If 160 mm tube length is correct for a thickness of 0·17 mm, the correct tube length for 0·19 mm will be about 150 mm and for 0·15 mm it will be about 180 mm.

After Using the Microscope

At the conclusion of work on the microscope, the lamp should be switched off, but with lamps carrying an intensity control, the intensity must be reduced to minimum *before* switching off. The body of the microscope should be raised until the objectives are well above the stage. The last specimen is removed, and a quick check made to see that the stage is clean and free from any spillage, immersion oil or loose particles if an uncovered object was used. The eye-lens of the eyepiece should be inspected for any dust, or grease from the eyelashes, which, if present should be cleaned off with lens tissue.

If either an objective or a condenser has been used in oil immersion, all traces of oil must be removed by repeated wiping with lens tissues until the glass is really clean, and many microscopists follow this by breathing on the glass and giving a final wipe to remove the moisture, claiming that this helps to preserve the delicate but important polish on the lenses. NEVER use any solvent, such as xylol, to clean an objective lens, for the cement which is used to reinforce the mounting of the front lens is usually softened by such solvent and the position of the front lens may be disturbed. As the polish on these lenses is so important, every effort must be made to avoid scratches. Consequently hard scrubbing even with lens tissue can be dangerous, and still more so, the use of a rag or handkerchief which may contain gritty dust particles should be avoided. Above all, the use of the tail-end of a laboratory coat as a cleaning implement (not unknown) must be prohibited.

When all has been checked and cleaned, the microscope should be covered with a plastic dust cover, if available, or returned to its case or to a cupboard. Whenever possible, some form of dust cover should be provided, as neither the microscope case nor a cupboard is dustproof. If a duster is used, and it may be better than nothing, see that it is free from loose dust by shaking it vigorously before draping it over the microscope: always remember that dust is the enemy of the microscope.

CHAPTER 6

Care and Maintenance

The microscope is an instrument of precision and is expensive. To maintain the precision and performance requires considerable attention to care and maintenance. The chief enemies of the microscope are dust, grease, moisture and accidental knocks, and these must be considered in relation to both the mechanical and the optical parts of the instrument.

If it is felt that the instrument requires cleaning, lubricating and adjustment, the wisest course is to call in the maker's service engineer who knows exactly how to deal with the parts, and who is provided with the correct lubricant for each. Should this be not possible, or in an emergency, the following notes will be of help.

If any moving part of a microscope becomes stiffer than usual, *never use force* to overcome the stiffness, as this could result in damage and expense. The cause of the trouble should be sought and the appropriate remedy applied.

Mechanical Parts

The moving parts are mostly slides or spindles in bearings, each provided with a suitable lubricant. The movements are adjusted to give free working, but without shake or loss, for such mechanical loss is reflected in very magnified form if it permits any movement between the specimen and the optical axis, or if it permits any disturbance of the position of the various optical units on the axis. If the microscope is allowed to become dusty, the dust settles into the lubricant, begins to dry it, and forms with it a very good grinding compound which will rapidly cut away metal surfaces and produce loose fits.

Slides. In the case of any of the slides, inspection will show if the lubricant is drying in which case the motion will be becoming stiffer. If inspection shows that the lubricant is looking darker the case becomes more serious. First-aid for a drying slide calls for the application of a small amount of light machine oil, not flooding the parts, to make the movement free again. But if darkening of the slide is seen, the whole slide must be carefully withdrawn, and then washed over with a brush or cloth dipped in xylol until the metal is quite clean. After drying, lubricant is applied and the parts reassembled. If possible, a lubricant obtained from the maker for such parts is much preferable to oil—it is usually a very light grease.

(*Important.* If a slide operated by rack and pinion is withdrawn from the microscope, very great care must be taken in replacing the slide, to ensure that the first tooth of the rack meets the teeth of the pinion gently, otherwise one or the other will be damaged by bending, and considerable trouble will result. As soon as the teeth come into contact the pinion should be turned slowly, in the right direction, to engage the teeth properly.)

Spindles offer a different problem. Although it may seem strange, the bearing surfaces of spindles are under very heavy loading, enough to break a film of oil and to allow metal surfaces to come into contact, resulting in tearing of the metal. Oil, therefore, is prohibited for the lubrication of spindles, and only a grease, developed for high loading, may be used. In view of this, every effort should be made to obtain assistance from the maker, and only in dire emergency should lubrication of a spindle, by grease, be attempted.

Racks and Pinions should always run dry—lubrication here is unnecessary and can only promote wear by holding dust particles which will grind away the metals.

The Nosepiece, if of the rotating type, requires grease on the centre cone, not oil.

Diaphragms. The leaves of an iris diaphragm should never be lubricated—they are made to run dry. The only lubrication required is an occasional drop of light oil through the slot in which the lever moves, to keep the circular moving part free.

Slipping Coarse Adjustment. After prolonged use it sometimes happens that, after focusing an objective, the object appears to go out of focus of its own accord. This is caused by the body of the microscope moving down under its own weight and calls for some re-adjustment. Never attempt a cure by making the teeth of the rack and pinion engage more deeply by, say, putting a packing piece behind the rack, or by bowing the rack outwards by bending. This can only cause more trouble. Most microscopes have some provision for increasing tension or pressure on the spindle of the pinion at the bearing point. It may be a pressure pad controlled by screws, or friction washers controlled by pressure from the end screws located in the centre of the milled heads, or some similar device. A properly adjusted coarse adjustment should require as much effort to raise the body as to lower it, with a smooth action, free from jerks even when operated very slowly. Any adjustment attempted by the user should aim at this.

Accidents. Should the microscope receive an accidental knock, or be knocked over on to the bench, it must be inspected all over to ensure that nothing has been bent or damaged. All the controls must rotate freely without wobble or eccentricity; slides should be free; the eyepiece tube must accept eyepieces freely; the mechanical stage should move freely and without shake or backlash; the nosepiece must rotate freely and engage positively when locating the objectives.

Any damage must be reported to whoever is in charge, and, to be on the safe side, the maker's engineer should be called in at once. If the user is not in charge of the microscope, there should be no attempt to conceal the accident. A continued use of a damaged instrument can only lead to more serious trouble.

Optical Parts

Dust, grease and moisture are the things to be avoided in any optical part of the microscope, and their location and remedy are best considered separately for each of the basic optical units— eyepiece, objective and condenser.

Moisture is troublesome in the form of condensation on the glass surfaces, and arises when a cold instrument is brought into a warm moist atmosphere. The only remedy is to wait until the whole microscope has had time to warm up and all condensation has disappeared, and it is useless to start wiping the surfaces—by the time the last one has been done, the first ones are again affected. Prevention is better than cure, and it is far more satisfactory to keep the instrument in a uniform atmosphere, preferably in the room where it is to be used.

In certain moist, tropical atmospheres, every effort should be made to keep the microscope as free from moisture as possible, by storing the instrument with efficient desiccators, to prevent deterioration of the parts and to delay the onset of fungoid growths. The problem of fungus on optical glass has never been properly solved —it may lie in the use of special glasses which appear less subject to this attack under these difficult conditions.

Definition and Resolution. There appears to be some confusion as to the meaning of these two terms. Resolution has been explained in the chapter on objectives, and concerns the ability of an objective to show small details separate from their surroundings. Definition concerns the clarity with which the final image is presented to the eye. For instance, an ·image produced by a good objective, in which all fine detail is perfectly resolved makes very poor viewing if there is a flood of light, producing glare, due to incorrect use of the condenser. Under these circumstances, there is a loss of definition. Good definition can be maintained only by good technique in setting-up the instrument, and by careful attention to the condition of the optical parts.

Eyepieces. The eye-lens is where *grease* is most likely to be found, deposited there either from a finger-print, which is always greasy, or from the eyelashes. The eye-lens is best cleaned by breathing on it and wiping with lens tissue. Several wipings may be necessary, and only rarely does the grease fail to respond to this treatment. In such an event, slightly moisten the tissue with xylol, wipe off the grease and follow with further wipings with dry tissue to remove all traces of the xylol.

Dust in the eyepiece can be very troublesome, especially if it is on a near plane of focus, and with the higher powers of eyepieces. If images of dust particles are observed in the field, rotate the eyepiece whilst looking through it, and, if the particles rotate, they are located in the eyepiece. If they appear in fairly sharp focus they are either on the bottom lens, or, if a graticule is in the eyepiece, on this graticule. Dust on the eye-lens cannot be seen when the microscope is being used. Remove the eyepiece and inspect the bottom lens in a good light, and dust may be seen on the outer face. Wipe the lens with tissue, until all particles seem to have gone, replace the eyepiece and repeat the rotation test. If any particles remain, they are probably on the inner face of the bottom lens. Holding the eyepiece vertical, eye-lens at the top, unscrew the bottom cell and place the eyepiece, open end down, on the bench. The inner face of the bottom lens is then wiped with tissue until it is free from dust. When clean, hold the cell with the inner face downwards, pick up the eyepiece, and, as quickly as possible screw the cell back into place. These precautions are taken to prevent additional dust from the air entering the eyepiece or falling on the newly cleaned surface.

It may happen that such wiping has failed to remove all particles. There is another method whereby obstinate particles, some of which have a great affinity for polished glass surfaces, may be removed. Take a soft camel-hair brush and make sure that it is completely free from grease (using some de-greasing agent if necessary) and wipe the bristles against the surface of a lighted electric light bulb. The bristles will then become electrically charged and will pick up even tiny particles from the glass when they are brought into contact. If prolonged cleaning is involved, repeat the wiping of the bristles against the bulb at frequent intervals. The brush should be kept for this purpose free from dust and grease, and the best way is to mount the brush in a rubber stopper which fits a test tube of the right length. The brush, kept in the test tube, is always clean and ready for use.

If the dust particles do not rotate with the eyepiece, and are well focused, they are most probably on the object slide, either on the top of the cover-glass or on the underside of the slide. This can be tested by moving the slide slightly during observation. Failing this, although they will not be sharply focused, they may be found on either the condenser or on the lamp. These will be discussed later.

Objectives. Contrary to expectation, dirt on an objective, with the exception of grease and moisture, may not entail a serious loss of definition. Dealing first with dust, there are only two lens faces where this may be found—the face of the front lens, and the rearmost face of the back lens. If the microscope is kept, as it should be, with the rotating nosepiece set at an objective position and not half way between two positions, and with an eyepiece (or a dust cap) always in position in the eyepiece tube, there should be very little dust deposited on the back lens. It cannot be seen when looking through the microscope, but if the objective is removed and held with the front lens close to the eye and with the back lens pointing towards a window or a light, dust particles may then be seen on the back lens, particularly if the objective be rotated during this inspection. Such particles are best removed by the camel-hair brush while holding the objective with the front lens uppermost. NEVER attempt to unscrew the components of an objective for cleaning or for any other purpose, as, without some optical control it will not be possible to reassemble the parts in the exact position which they previously occupied and the performance of the objective may well be spoilt.

Dust on the front lens is best removed by the brush. Great care must be taken not to scratch the polish of the front lens by rubbing dust particles, some of which may be harder than glass, over the surface if anything but the brush is used. Lens tissue, used delicately, is the best alternative, but no hard rubbing is allowed.

Much more serious to the performance of the objective is any grease or moisture on the front lens, which will result in a quite noticeable reduction in image quality (i.e. loss of definition). The appearance of the image is usually rather hazy and milky, instead of being clear and crisp, and no amount of focusing or light control will cure it. Traces of immersion oil on the front lens are a potential source of danger, as exposure to the atmosphere will allow dust particles to settle on the oil and subsequent removal by a brush is not possible. Wiping with lens tissue, unless done very carefully, will make the dust particles scratch the glass.

In all cases like these, clean lens tissue must be used again and again until the glass is really clean. In obstinate cases of grease there may be some still visible after such treatment. If so, very slight moistening of the tissue with xylol is permissible provided that it is wiped off immediately and that there is not enough xylol on the tissue to really wet the glass. After the xylol, polishing with clean tissue follows, and, perhaps, a final polishing after *breathing* on the glass.

It can happen that balsam from a newly prepared specimen can get on to the front lens, and, if overlooked, can harden there. This cannot then be removed by wiping, and the only remedy is to use xylol in small amounts on the tissue, repeated as often as necessary until all traces of the balsam are removed, followed by polishing, as before, with clean tissue. But, as before, only the minimum amount of xylol must be used.

A badly scratched front lens can produce loss of definition similar to that due to a film of grease on the surface, and such an objective must be returned to the maker for repolishing or for a new front lens.

It is still possible that the old type of evaporating immersion oil has been used and not thoroughly removed after use. This will set quite hard and will hold dangerous dust particles, and will defy removal by wiping. It can be dissolved by xylol but this involves the use of too much xylol for the safety of the front lens and must be discouraged. The only safe way is to dissolve the dried immersion oil in fresh oil of the same type. Stand the objective on the bench, lens uppermost, and apply fresh oil to the front lens, and leave for some time. It will be found that the hard deposit has been dissolved, and cleaning the front lens then follows the procedures outlined above. Never attempt to scrape off such a deposit—almost certainly the front lens will thereby be scratched.

Binocular Bodies, through neglect or careless handling, may require attention to remove dust or grease. If the eyepieces have been removed and the eyepiece tubes left open and unprotected, dust can settle on the faces of the prisms below the eyepieces. This is best removed by using the camel-hair brush with the body inverted so that the open end of the eyepiece tubes points downwards. By doing this, any dust particles displaced by the brush will tend to fall out of the body.

Careless handling may result in a fingerprint on the correcting lens at the bottom of the body. Wiping with lens tissue will remove this safely.

Under no circumstances may a binocular body be opened to give access to the faces of prisms inside the body. Displacement of the prisms is very easy, and to correct such displacement involves a return to the maker for realignment on a collimator.

Condensers. Dust and grease on condenser lenses cannot be seen through the miscroscope, but may give rise to scattering of light producing glare. If there is dust and grease on the top lens of the condenser, removal is easy by wiping with lens tissue. If on the bottom lens, larger particles, being near the back focal plane, may result in darker patches being seen in the field of view which alter in size and density as the condenser is put in and out of focus. They are removed, as usual, with lens tissue, or, in obstinate cases, by the camel-hair brush. Grease, fingerprints and similar blemishes are dealt with in similar manner.

Mirrors. Dust and grease on the mirror are of little importance in relation to definition, and are easily removed with lens tissue. If, however, a *surface aluminized mirror* is involved, very great care must be taken to avoid scratching the rather delicate polished surface, and the camel-hair brush is obviously very much safer than lens tissue. Because of the delicacy of the surface, handling of a surface aluminized mirror should always be done with care, by holding the outside rim between finger and thumb, and never permitting a finger to touch the surface and leave a greasy deposit. Removal of grease is very difficult without spoiling the mirror, but a very light and gentle application of some de-greasing fluid on a very soft applicator may be attempted.

It should be noted that a newly polished surface aluminized mirror will lose its reflectivity fairly rapidly until about 60% of the original reflectivity is reached. From then onwards, there is very little change, but, eventually, due to the atmosphere, dust and grease, the reflectivity shows another large decrease. When this happens, the mirror should go back to the maker for repolishing. In fact, a regular repolishing, at suitable intervals, can be recommended for these mirrors.

Lamps and Filters. An occasional source of trouble, difficult to trace, lies in a mark, such as a finger-print on the glass envelope of a lamp bulb at the point where the light is emerging towards the microscope. Such a blemish can produce a hazy, darkish mark in the field, which no tests, such as have been described, will locate, and this may be much more noticeable in photomicrography than in visual microscopy. The remedy is obvious—wait until the bulb is cold, and then polish off the offending blemish.

If the lamp has a condenser lens, the outside surfaces should be kept free from dust and grease, and, also, any filters, before they are inserted, should be inspected, and, if necessary, wiped clean before use. To prevent grease on filters, they should always be handled by their edges. With filters and lamp condensers, avoidance of scratches is desirable, if not actually necessary, and reasonable precautions in cleaning, and in storage, will ensure this.

To sum up this chapter, it will be seen that the careful handling of a microscope while in use, and reasonable precautions while out of use, will ensure a long useful life for the instrument with the minimum of trouble. Such procedures as have been suggested for cleaning and maintenance should be regarded as for use in maintaining the peak of condition. But, even with every care, any precision instrument can, in time, develop wear in the vital parts, and it cannot be stressed too much that *regular servicing* by the trained engineers of the maker will do much to extend the useful life of the microscope. Such servicing facilities are now generally available everywhere, not only in the country of origin, but in many foreign countries where the makers have now established such facilities.

PART 2

Advanced Microscopy

CHAPTER 7

Micrometry

Micrometry is the art of measuring detail in an object when viewed through a microscope, and is, therefore, being an optical method, distinct from mechanical measurement which can be done only at very low magnification.

Unit of Measurement

The unit for micrometry is one micron, usually written as 1 μ, and which is equal to 0·001 mm. Some workers prefer another unit, the angstrom unit, usually written as Å. 10,000 Å equal 1 μ.

In micrometry, the microscope is set up in such a manner that not only is the object in focus, but, superimposed on the object, a series of lines, squares or other shapes is equally visible, and comparison is made between the object being measured and the number of lines, squares, etc., apparently covered by the object. The lines, etc., are engraved or photographically reproduced on a glass disc which is mounted inside the eyepiece at the focal point of the eye-lens, that is, on the diaphragm inside the eyepiece, at which point the image from the objective is also focused, so that the two can be viewed simultaneously. The disc of lines, etc., is called a *graticule*, or, in older books, an *eyepiece micrometer*.

It will be appreciated that the size of the object, viewed as indicated, can be recorded in terms of so many eyepiece divisions, or squares, but this is of little value, except in comparison work where one object can be compared in size with another, and it is necessary to give an exact value, in microns, to each eyepiece division. This calls for calibration against some known size, and the usual method is to use a *stage micrometer*, which is a 3 in. × 1 in. slide having at its centre some parallel lines very accurately ruled with a diamond point at intervals of 0·1 mm (100 μ) and 0·01 mm (10 μ) or of 0·01 and 0·001 in.

The eye is capable of focusing objects, and this capacity is called accommodation. If, when setting up a microscope for micrometry, this accommodation is used in the focusing of the graticule there will exist a condition of parallax. The effect of this, during comparison or counting the size of the object against the lines of the graticule, may cause the graticule lines to appear to move or "drift" over the object due to inadvertent movement of the head of the operator (for there is no physical contact between the operator and the eyepiece), and the original start-point for the count will have moved, invalidating the result. It is essential, therefore, to eliminate all parallax due to this accommodation of the eye—and the younger the eye, the greater is the available accommodation.

For this reason, one must discourage the rather common practice of dropping the graticule on to the diaphragm of an ordinary eyepiece. It may happen in a few cases that when the cell holding the eye-lens is screwed home the graticule is in sharp focus. If it is not, it may happen that by unscrewing the cell a few turns, accurate focusing can be obtained. But, more often, the cell cannot be unscrewed enough to do this, or, in other cases, the cell would require to be screwed further into the eyepiece, which is impossible, so that for all these reasons, an ordinary eyepiece is unsuitable.

The only reliable method is to use a *micrometer eyepiece* in which the eye-lens is mounted in a sliding tube, giving a large range of focusing. Using such an eyepiece, the technique to eliminate parallax is for the operator to put the objective out of focus; then slide the eye-lens in or out until the graticule lines are perfectly sharp; then focus the objective until the object is equally sharp—these steps to be done in that order. As a test, it will now be found that any movement of the eye over the eye-lens fails to show any movement of the graticule lines over the object—they seem to be locked together. The size of the object can now be studied in relation to the graticule, and the result recorded as so many eyepiece divisions.

While eyepiece graticules are catalogued as being "10 mm divided into 100 parts of 100 μ", or "sides of squares 1 mm", and so on, these values are really of no significance and, indeed, can give rise to confusion if they are so read without taking into consideration the important matter of calibration, for the actual value of the graticule divisions in relation to the object being measured varies according to the power of the objective and the tube length at which it is being used.

Calibration

Calibration can be effected either by exchanging a stage micrometer for the object after its size has been recorded in terms of eye-

piece divisions or before any micrometry is done, a record being
made of the value of each eyepiece division under set conditions of
use.

Whichever way is adopted, the procedure is as follows:

With the objective out of focus, set the eye-lens of the micrometer eyepiece to focus sharply the graticule divisions.

With a stage micrometer on the stage, focus the objective until
the lines on the stage micrometer are sharply focused. Move the
micrometer until one of its lines is in exact coincidence with a
numbered line on the graticule. Count how many eyepiece divisions
cover the space between the selected line on the micrometer and the
next one. If the space on the micrometer is 100 μ and it is found
that, say, 33 eyepiece divisions exactly match this space, then the

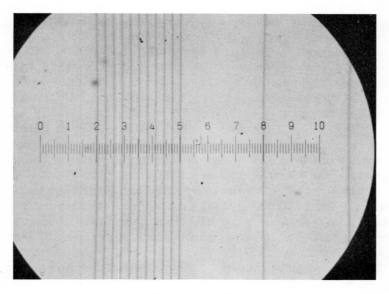

Fig. 17. Graticule calibration

value of 1 eyepiece division is 100 μ ÷ 33 = 3·03 μ, and so on. In the
above figure, the short, numbered lines are those of the eyepiece
graticule. The long lines crossing the whole field are those of the
stage micrometer. The large spaces on the micrometer measure
100 μ across, and one such space is subdivided into 10 spaces

each of 10 μ. As set up, it will be seen that a micrometer line has been brought into coincidence with the graticule line No. 5 and that 30 eyepiece divisions, to line No. 8, exactly cover the 100 μ space.

In micrometry, if it is to be of real value, great accuracy is worth while. In the example quoted above it may happen that not 33 but, say, 32 and an estimated $\frac{2}{3}$ of a division, or, say 33 and an estimated $\frac{1}{4}$ of a division, cover the space of 100 μ. This estimation can clearly lead to inaccuracy, being a personal estimation which may differ between several observers. The need for this estimation can be eliminated, as follows.

It will be remembered that the nominal magnification of an objective is correct only at a particular tube length, and that it is increased or decreased as the tube length is increased or decreased above or below the selected length, usually 160 mm in British and American microscopes. If, in our example, it were found that $32\frac{2}{3}$ eyepiece divisions equal 100 μ, a small increase in the magnification of the objective, by extending the tube length beyond 160 mm would make the 100 μ cover exactly 33 eyepiece divisions. Similarly, if $33\frac{1}{4}$ eyepiece divisions equal 100 μ at 160 mm tube length, a small decrease in the tube length below 160 mm will make 33 divisions equal 100 μ.

By always using the tube length to eliminate fractions, much greater accuracy will be obtained, without any significant reduction in the performance of the objective, but it is essential that in recording the results of calibration the particular objective and the tube length which was used be specified. Thereafter, before micrometry is started, after mounting the calibrated objective and presetting the tube length to the calibration figure, direct readings in microns can be obtained without further trouble, and with considerable accuracy.

Owing to optical imperfections towards the periphery of the field, micrometry should be done, as far as possible, in the centre of the field, and this applies equally to calibration.

It so happens, without any sound optical reason, that the value in microns per eyepiece division for different objectives, approximates the focal length in millimetres of the objective, and this may be used as a rough guide to show if the calibration is approximately accurate and that, say, a decimal point has not been misplaced. If they be so regarded, i.e. as a very rough guide, the following figures can be quoted, but they will vary, of course, with different objectives of the same nominal magnification, and, also, with the actual tube length used:

16 mm objective × 10   1 eyepiece division = 15 μ
4 mm objective × 40   1 eyepiece division = 3·3 μ
2 mm objective × 100   1 eyepiece division = 1·5 μ

It must be emphasized that these values are entirely fortuitous, and that they are not to be used as a substitute for correct calibration.

While the use of the eyepiece graticule is, by far, the commonest method of micrometry, there are other methods available and these will now be discussed.

Screw Micrometer Eyepiece (or Filar Eyepiece)

This is a special measuring eyepiece (by Beck and others) and consists essentially of two very fine lines or webs parallel to each other which run across the microscope field. While one line is fixed towards the side of the field, the other is movable and can be traversed over the field by an external rotating head, from contact with the fixed line to the other side of the field. Across the bottom of the field is an opaque strip whose edge is patterned with sawlike teeth. One rotation of the control head will traverse the moving line from the point of one tooth to the point of the next. As the control head has a drum with 100 divisions, the movement of the moving line can be read to one hundredth of a tooth spacing.

But, as before, except for comparison work a value in microns must be given to the drum divisions, and calibration against a stage micrometer must be done. After careful focusing of the eye-lens to make the lines quite sharp, the moving line is made to coincide with the fixed line, and one line of the stage micrometer is set to coincide at the same point. If the 100 μ spacing of the stage micrometer is being used, the number of teeth and drum divisions beyond the last tooth required to cover the 100 μ space are noted, also the tube length at which calibration is being made. From this recorded number a value in microns per drum division is easily calculated, and, as before, this value will hold good for every occasion on which the calibrated objective is used again at the recorded tube length.

With this system, errors due to estimated fractions are eliminated, and it is found easier to use with the fixed and movable lines superimposed. One edge of the object to be measured is set against these superimposed lines; the moving line is then moved until it reaches the opposite edge of the object. The distance traversed will be so many "teeth" plus so many hundredths as shown on the drum, and from the calibration record, this result can be translated into reading in microns.

By Projection

Using a darkened room or cabinet, the microscope can be set up in the vertical position and the image of the object projected on to a horizontal translucent screen and the size of the object marked thereon. By substituting the stage micrometer for the object and projecting the lines of the micrometer and marking these on the screen, the use of dividers enables one to measure the object against the micrometer lines.

As an alternative to the above, the vertical microscope can have a projection prism mounted above the eyepiece and the images are then thrown on to a vertical screen, which is probably easier for drawing and measurement.

The third possibility is to use the microscope in the horizontal position and project direct from the eyepiece on to the vertical screen, without the prism.

Any of these methods eliminates the use of the micrometer eyepiece and the graticule.

By Photography

If the enlarged projected image of a stage micrometer is photographed, very accurate determination can be made of the space on the photograph occupied by, say, 100 μ. If, subsequently, any object is photographed under identical conditions, the magnification on the photograph will be the same and it is possible to measure any dimension in terms of the size of the photograph of the stage micrometer, thus eliminating the use of the micrometer eyepiece and graticule. This method is useful when dealing with irregular shaped objects, or such things as the length of curved fibres, wires, etc.

Special Graticules

In addition to the graticules already described (linear scales or squares over the field) there has been developed a large range of special markings for specific purposes. Particle sizing is, today, an important function of the microscope and frequent use is made of the Patterson and of the Porton graticules. These both have areas of the field covered by rectangles to assist in the counting of particles, and, in addition, there are series of dots and circles of known size, against which the size of the particles can be compared. These dots and circles carry numbers indicating their diameter in microns when the graticule is used with an objective of specified magnification.

There is the Whipple graticule which combines squares of various sizes, and this is in frequent use for bacterial counts in milk.

Amongst the less frequently used graticules are those with concentric circles, a protractor half-circle, and a protractor full circle, both divided in degrees and both these protractors are used for angular measurements.

The Image Shearing Eyepiece

All the methods of micrometry described so far involve the comparison of the object to be measured with a fixed scale. This does involve an element of personal judgment, and such methods are quite unusable in cases where the object is moving or drifting over the field.

A new system is coming into use and is called "image shearing", in which the image of an object is compared with itself. The following description is of the Watson Image Shearing Eyepiece which has been developed for this purpose. As will be seen from Fig. 18 the instrument consists of a box with a stem which fits into the eyepiece tube of the microscope. At the top of the box is a viewing eyepiece, and at the side is a control head, a digital counter and a drum and vernier. Internally, as shown in Fig. 19, is a system of lenses, a prism, mirrors, and a dichroic beam splitter, and this latter is the heart of the system. The beam splitter produces two images of the object to be measured, each image being in a contrasting colour—red and green. By rotation of the control head, the mirrors are moved and these images gradually separate from each other until a position is reached where there are two distinct images, red and green, without overlap and without any space between them. The production of the two coloured images and their separation is known as image shearing. Where there is overlap, shearing is incomplete; when there are two separate images, just touching, but without overlap, the state of full shear has been achieved. Figure 20 indicates these steps from zero shear to full shear.

The control head moves the mirrors which separate the images and the amount of movement required to do this depends on the size of the object, the smaller the object, the smaller the movement. This amount of movement is recorded on the counter and the vernier. It has been found that operators with no experience of this system are able to judge the position of full shear with remarkable accuracy and this accuracy is repeatable. This is probably

Fig. 18. Watson image shearing eyepiece

because of the brilliancy of the images (it is claimed that the loss of light by absorption in the system is as low as 3%) and because of the contrast between the unsheared part of the object, which is seen in its original colour (black, for instance in the case of an opaque particle) and the coloured sheared images. As long as there

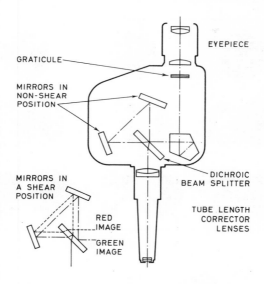

Fig. 19. Optical system, image shearing eyepiece

is any overlap, a residue of the black remains, and when full shear has been passed, the clear space between the coloured images, no matter how small, is clearly visible.

As with all systems of micrometry, it is necessary to calibrate the instrument against a stage micrometer for each particular objective and tube length; this calibration then gives a value in microns per division of the counter—the vernier can sub-divide this division value into tenths. The procedure is to focus the viewing eyepiece on to the graticule which defines the direction of shear, and the objective on to the lines of the stage micrometer. Having zeroed the instrument by checking that no coloured image is visible alongside the lines of the micrometer, the reading of the counter and vernier are recorded. The control head is then rotated, in either direction, and the two coloured images of the lines will be seen to separate from the lines and travel away from them. Eventually each coloured

6

line will coincide with the next stage line, and all colour disappears. Full shear has been achieved, and the new reading of the counter and vernier is recorded. One subtracted from the other gives the number of divisions and tenths required to shear a space of, say, 100 μ on the stage micrometer, and simple calculation gives the value in microns per division.

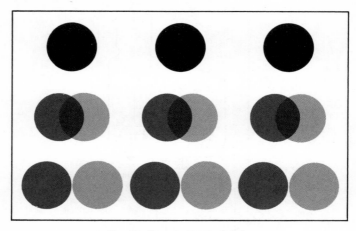

Fig. 20. Steps in image shearing

To indicate the order of measurement obtainable with this device, the following table is given, by permission of W. Watson & Sons Ltd.

Objective Magnification and Focal Length		Largest Measurable Dimension, Approx.	Approx. Value of one Division of Drum Vernier
×4	40 mm	0·560 mm (0·0220 in.)	1·10 μ (0·0000440 in.)
×10	16 mm	0·225 mm (0·0088 in.)	0·45 μ (0·0000180 in.)
×20	8 mm	0·110 mm (0·0043 in.)	0·22 μ (0·0000086 in.)
×40	4 mm	0·056 mm (0·0022 in.)	0·11 μ (0·0000044 in.)
×100	2 mm	0·025 mm (0·0010 in.)	0·05 μ (0·0000020 in.)

To use the image shearing eyepiece, the microscope is set up critically with the eyepiece in position, and the control head is adjusted to remove all shear, i.e. coloured images, and the counter is read and recorded (this is usually at 50 in standard instruments). A single image of the object is now seen. The control head is now rotated in either direction, and the two coloured images appear, gradually separating from the original, and rotation is continued until full shear is obtained. The counter and vernier are now read again, and from this number is subtracted the original one. Previous calibration has given a value in microns per division of the counter, and the actual size is thus obtained. For greater accuracy, the control head is reversed and the shearing reduced to zero and then carried out in the opposite direction with a reversal of the coloured images, and again, at full shear the counter is read. The true size measured is the mean of the two results.

As many objects are of irregular shape, they can be measured in any direction, say long axis and short axis, by simple rotation of the instrument in the eyepiece tube to alter the direction of shear, the direction being indicated by the graticule below the viewing eyepiece.

It is possible to do differential size work with this instrument, with particles, fibres and similar objects. The critical size is set on the counter, and random fields of the specimen are examined. Any particles, etc., which show full shear are of the critical size; those which show partial shear (overlap of the images) are larger than the critical; any which show space between the coloured images are smaller than the critical. Hence a very rapid determination of percentage size distribution can be made.

The Ehrlich Eyepiece

This is a special eyepiece in which the usual circular diaphragm which limits the field is replaced by a square diaphragm which is adjustable from an external control to produce squares of varying sizes, with visible notches on the sides to indicate squares of specific area.

It is used for estimating the relative proportion of red and white blood corpuscles in dry preparations. The usual magnification is × 6.

CHAPTER 8

Dark-Ground Illumination

There are many objects which, because of their transparency, cannot be seen easily by the methods using transmitted light which have been discussed earlier. In such cases, an increase in contrast between the object and its surroundings is of more help than sheer resolution, and dark-ground illumination is used to provide this contrast.

Hitherto, in speaking of the function of the condenser, stress has been laid on obtaining maximum light through the condenser into the objective. In dark-ground illumination the opposite is the aim, i.e. to prevent any light from the condenser entering the objective. If there is no light there will be darkness, and this darkness provides the black background against which the specimen is examined. If the condenser can produce a hollow cone of light of great obliquity, the light rays emerging from the condenser can be focused on to the specimen, and after crossing in the plane of focus they continue outside the front lens of the objective. But if at the point of focus there is any object which can reflect or scatter light, then some of this scattered light will enter the front lens and produce an image of the object which is then seen illuminated against a black background. This is dark-ground illumination.

Low Power Dark-Ground Illumination

With low power objectives, up to, and including the 16 mm, dark-ground illumination is comparatively easy because of the long working distance of the objective. A simple Abbe condenser used complete, or with the top lens removed for very low power objectives, is very suitable. All the central rays are stopped by an opaque disc, or "patch stop" which is fitted into the filter carrier below the condenser mount, and an annular cone of light is produced which can be focused on to the object without any direct rays entering the objective. The object will reflect or scatter light from its outer surface or envelope and some of this scattered light then enters the objective and the object is seen as a silvery object on a black background.

The size of the disc, or patch stop, varies with the power of the objective, and it can be determined as follows: If the eyepiece is removed when the objective is at its correct working distance, i.e. when focused on to the object, closing the iris diaphragm of the condenser will produce an image of the diaphragm seen in the back lens of the objective when viewed from the top of the body tube.

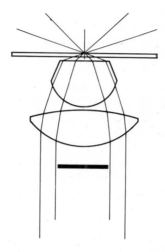

Fig. 21. Low power dark-ground illumination

An opening of the diaphragm can be found such that the back lens is almost filled with light leaving the diaphragm just visible at the margins of the lens. The diameter of the opening of the diaphragm thus obtained is that of the required patch stop for this objective, and, if a set of metal stops is available, the nearest smaller size should be selected.

A more convenient way of obtaining dark ground for these conditions is the use of the Traviss Stop (Beck; Watson). This consists of a reversed iris diaphragm in which the leaves are mounted at the centre and can be expanded to discs of varying size by movement of the control lever. Mounted in the filter carrier, with the objective in focus, the leaves are expanded to eliminate all direct light and produce the best possible dark background.

The types of objects best seen with low power dark-ground illumination include:

Almost transparent algae, infusoria, rotifera, and the larger diatoms—all found in water.

Small crustaceans, mites and similar objects.

Foraminifera.

Slide-agglutinations.

Cells and casts in urinary deposits.

Rheinberg Discs

An interesting and rather spectacular variation of low power dark-ground illumination, which has gone out of fashion, is worth mentioning. In the system described above, the central rays are stopped out to provide a black background while the object is illuminated by white light. The Rheinberg discs consist of discs of coloured material (such as celluloid) with central patches of a contrasting colour, e.g. green with red, or blue with yellow, etc. The inner patch provides the colour of the background while the outer part gives the colour with which the object is illuminated. Such colour contrasts can, in some cases, make the details of the object more visible with the removal of the glare sometimes found with white objects on a black background and, for exhibition work, can be very attractive.

Setting Up

Because of the difficulty of setting up to provide the black background, this simple low power dark-ground illumination is best confined to the 16 mm and lower powers of objectives with N.A. not exceeding 0·3. Having determined the size of the stop to be used, the microscope is set up in the usual way for axial illumination and, after the objective has been focused, the filter carrier holding the patch stop is swung into position. Small changes in the focus of the condenser should be tried to produce the maximum brightness of the object and the maximum darkness of the background. During this work, the diaphragm of the condenser must be kept fully open.

High Power Dark-Ground Illumination

Most of the work with dark-ground illumination is done with high power objectives, especially the oil-immersion objectives, in the observation of living organisms, to see their size and shape and motility, if any, and, in venereology for the examination of spiro-chetes and trichomonas.

Because these objectives have very short working distances, the system described for low powers is quite unsuitable as it cannot supply rays of sufficient obliquity to avoid entry into the objective. A special dark-ground condenser is necessary. One well-known type was called the Paraboloid, but this has largely been replaced by the concentric or Zonal type.

Figure 22 shows how the emerging rays are obtained by internal reflections, first from the silvered hemisphere, and then from the

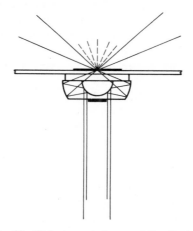

Fig. 22. High power dark-ground illumination

lenticular curved walls. For the purpose of the illustration the emerging rays are drawn with less obliquity than in actual fact, for they emerge at such obliquity that it is possible to use objectives of very high power, and, hence, of very short working distance, and still avoid entry into the front lens.

While it is possible to design a dark-ground condenser which will prevent the entry of light even with objectives of N.A. 1·30 or 1·37 (the Nelson Cassegrain Condenser (Watson) was such a con-denser), these condensers are difficult to use and have almost dis-appeared. The modern method is to use condensers which will give dark ground up to objective apertures of N.A. 1·0 or 1·15. With greater aperture, light can enter the objective, but is prevented from passing by means of a Funnel stop or an in-built iris dia-phragm within the objective. Use of these devices does, in fact, reduce the aperture of the objective and its resolving power, but such sacrifice of resolution is more than compensated by the contrast obtained by dark ground, and by the comparative ease of manipulation.

As before, under these conditions, no direct light from the condenser passes through the objective, giving dark ground. If any object is present at the point of focus and such object is capable of reflecting light then some of this reflected light will pass through the objective and form an image of the object, which is then seen as a silvery object against a black background.

Because the field of view of these high power objectives (focal lengths 3·6 mm and 2 mm) is so very small, it is essential that the focal point of the dark-ground condenser is located within that field of view. Hence it is essential that the condenser be mounted in some form of centring mount or in a substage with centring controls.

It will be realized that this combination of very high power objectives and these special dark-ground condensers utilizes rays of light of very wide angle, well beyond the "critical angle". Hence all air between the condenser and the specimen slide, and between the slide and the objective must be eliminated by the use of immersion oil.

As only a very tiny fraction of the light fed into the system, that scattered or reflected by very small objects, actually goes through the microscope, a light source of far higher intensity than that of the ordinary bench lamp must be employed. Suitable sources are the high intensity lamps used in substage Köhler illumination units; other Köhler illumination units external to the microscope; the Pointolite Lamp; the Ribbon Filament Lamp; the Carbon Arc; the M.E.D. Mercury Discharge Lamp. It is always an advantage to increase the contrast and visibility by using the microscope in a dark room or in a very shaded position away from windows and room lighting. Some workers have built a plywood hood to screen the microscope and the operator's head from external light.

Focusing and Slide Thickness

The emerging rays from the dark-ground condenser come to a point of focus at a little distance above the top of the condenser, and having crossed at this point, proceed outwards. As these rays are in the form of a hollow annulus, at positions both above and below the point of focus there is a ring of light with a black central area.

The art of using the condenser is to position it so that the focal point coincides exactly with the plane on which the object is located, and as the object is on the upper surface of the glass slide, the thickness of this slide has to be considered.

Referring to Fig. 23, it will be seen that after focusing the condenser through the immersion oil which joins it to the underside of

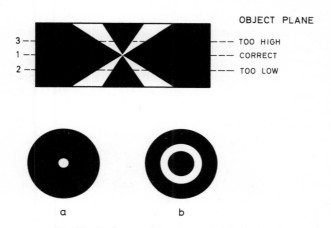

Fig. 23. Dark-ground focusing and slide thickness

the slide, the light comes to a focal point as at (1) and (a), which is where the object lies.

If, however, the slide thickness is so great that the condenser cannot be focused high enough to achieve this before there is actual physical contact between the upper face of the condenser and the underside of the slide, then the focal point lies below the plane of the object. The object is, consequently, illuminated by a ring of light with a black centre, as at (3) and (b), and, as this black centre is usually far larger than the field of the objective, nothing can be seen.

On the other hand, if the slide thickness is much reduced, the opposite effect is obtained, as at (2) and (b), and, to maintain oil contact between condenser and slide, the condenser cannot be lowered enough to bring the focal point down to the plane of the object—again producing the ring of light with the dark centre.

In view of all this, slide thickness is of great importance. Most makers of modern dark-ground condensers specify that they must be used through slides 1·2 mm thick, and the supply houses are able to offer boxes of selected slides of thicknesses ranging from 1·0 mm to about 1·3 mm. It is probably better to select slides by micrometer measurement as near as possible to 1·2 mm as most condensers will not work through much more than 1·3 mm while with slides less than 1·0 mm it becomes very difficult to maintain oil contact. One method of doing this has been suggested—if the slide is very thin, one or more cover glasses can be applied to the top of the condenser, being "cemented" there by immersion oil, to build up sufficient height to maintain oil contact when the condenser is focused at the plane of the object.

Condensers have been made (Beck; Cooke) with a focusing adjustment whereby it is possible to produce dark ground irrespective of slide thickness, at all events within a range of about 0·5–1·5 mm. These are obviously useful, but the majority of workers use the simpler condensers with pre-selected slides.

Requirements

Summarizing the foregoing, the requirements for high power dark-ground illumination are as follows:
1. Special dark-ground condenser.
2. Centring mount.
3. Funnel stop or iris diaphragm in the objective.
4. Light of high intensity.
5. Slides of 1·2 mm thickness.
6. Oil-immersion contact throughout.

Setting Up

A surprising number of workers seem to dread having to set up a microscope for dark-ground illumination, in view of much wasted time with previous attempts. The cause of this is generally that they have attempted to do all the setting up with the oil-immersion objective. But a moment's thought will show that if the condenser is not accurately focused, the objective will be searching in the comparatively large pool of darkness within the ring of light, while, even if the condenser were properly focused but not accurately centred, the disc of illumination may well be outside the field of the objective.

The correct method is to use the 16 mm objective for setting up because of its large field of view. The procedure is as follows:

1. Direct the light into the bottom of the condenser, with the condenser diaphragm fully open. By viewing the top of the condenser, it can be seen when the whole top is evenly illuminated.

2. Apply a generous drop of immersion oil free from air bubbles, to the top of the condenser, and using the focusing control of the sub-stage, lower the condenser until the top is below the level of the stage.

3. Put the slide into position on the stage. If stage clips are available, use them to hold the slide down.

4. Raise the condenser until the oil makes contact with the underside of the slide, and continue slowly until the oil spreads out to the margin of the top of the condenser.

5. Using the 16 mm objective, focus the objective on to the specimen on the slide. In all probability there will be seen a ring of illuminated objects (particles, organisms, etc.) with a black centre, as in Fig. 23(b).

6. By using the centring controls, adjust the position of the condenser until this ring of light is central to the field.

7. Now focus the condenser very delicately up or down to reduce the ring of light, as in Fig. 23(b), to a solid disc of light, as in Fig. 23(a), of the smallest possible diameter.

8. Raise the body of the microscope and rotate the nosepiece to bring the oil-immersion objective into position. Apply a drop of immersion oil to the slide above the centre of the condenser. Lower the objective into the oil, and, very gently, complete the focusing. This should present a perfect dark-ground picture.

Preparation of Material

The ideal specimen for dark-ground illumination should consist of particles or organisms well separated by clear spaces, and of one layer thick. The spaces provide the black background against which the illuminated objects are seen in maximum contrast. If all the objects are not in the same plane, those above and below the plane of focus will scatter sufficient light to mask the dark spaces, and so destroy the black background. If the objects are too closely packed, there will be insufficient black background visible to promote the contrast. Consequently, all preparations must be very dilute to give good separation, and the films must be very thin to provide one layer of objects.

Air bubbles, either in the film or in the immersion oil, act as very high reflecting spheres which will scatter enough light to spoil the dark-ground effect even if the bubbles are out of the field of view. They must be avoided at all costs. Dust particles anywhere, also smears of grease, will also scatter light and tend to destroy the black background. In the application of the immersion oil, reflection from air bubbles can frequently be seen even before looking through the objective, and the only safe thing to do is to wipe off the oil and start again. All grease on slides, cover glasses and condenser top must be carefully removed before work commences, and it is a good plan to keep slides, of the correct thickness, and cover glasses, all of which have been carefully de-greased, in special containers with liquid, maintained dust-free by suitable covers. In making the films, avoid, as far as possible, exposure to the dust of the atmosphere, and keep everything covered until the moment of use.

Evaporation of the fluid of the film from the edges of the cover glass will cause a flow of fluid across the field with drifting of the objects. This must not be confused with the natural motility of certain organisms, and can generally be distinguished because evaporation drift is in one constant direction, while motile organisms move at random. If prolonged observations are to be made, evaporation can be prevented by surrounding the area in which the film is to be placed by a very light application of vaseline or other light grease, to which the cover glass can be pressed to effect a seal. There will then be no fluid flow or drifting of the objects across the field.

Special Condensers

In addition to the focusing type of dark-ground condensers mentioned above, there are two others which can be used for dark-ground work.

The Trilux Condenser (Baker) is a combination condenser which, according to its setting, provides bright field, dark-ground or phase-contrast conditions. In its dark-ground setting, it functions on the lines of the foregoing description.

The Heine Condenser (Leitz) is another combination condenser also providing bright field, dark-ground and phase-contrast conditions, but, in this condenser, the progress from one form of illumination to another is obtained during actual observation of the specimen and the progress is continual, and not in steps. Consequently, the observer can examine a particular specimen by all three methods at will, and can go backwards and forwards from one to the other without interruption of viewing. In between the three major settings are intermediate ones which, on the one hand provide increased contrast in bright field images and, on the other, increase contrast in dark-ground images. This condenser must be used with the special objectives produced by the maker for this purpose.

CHAPTER 9

Phase-Contrast Microscopy

When instructing on the subject and demonstrating the equipment, it is found that phase-contrast microscopy is probably the most difficult technique to understand and the most difficult to explain. Yet this valuable technique is becoming more widely adopted; users of the microscope need some understanding of what lies behind it, and many students need this information which is required by their syllabus.

This chapter is an attempt to set out the basic principles in very simplified form and to build up from them an explanation of what is happening. Naturally, in such simplification, a great deal of the more intricate optical problems of a very complex topic is omitted. There are many books and published articles on the subject which may be consulted by those eager to learn more.

Phase-contrast microscopy is a technique which enables us to see very transparent objects, which are almost invisible by ordinary transmitted light, in clear detail and in good contrast to their surroundings, and to detect very small differences in thickness and/or density within the object. This is achieved without altering the object by staining or other processing, so that we see living cells and tissues, in their natural state.

Phase-contrast microscopy was developed comparatively recently by a German optical worker, Prof. F. Zernike. The original papers were published in 1942 and since then there has been a continuous expansion of the uses of the technique in many fields of microscopy.

We can see an object either because it has a different colour from its surroundings or, if it is not coloured, because it has a different optical density or a different thickness than its surroundings. A familiar object in the laboratory is a glass bottle of immersion oil with a glass dropper rod. If we look at the part of the rod which is in the air above the level of the oil, we see the rod clearly because its optical density differs from that of the surrounding air. But, where the rod is immersed in the oil, it is quite invisible because the optical densities of the oil and of the rod are the same. Were there a slight difference in optical density, the rod would be barely visible by transmitted light, but phase-contrast would use this slight difference to build-up an easily seen rod.

As a basis for understanding phase-contrast, certain optical principles must be clearly understood.

Wave Formation

Light is a form of energy which is transmitted in straight lines in the form of waves. This can be illustrated as shown in Fig. 24 where the waves oscillate above and below a datum line. Distance between

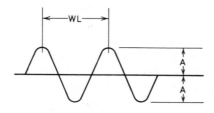

WL = WAVE-LENGTH
A = AMPLITUDE

Fig. 24. Wave formation

peaks or troughs is a measure of wave-length, or colour. Heights above or below the datum are a measure of amplitude or brightness.

Interference

When two sets of waves, or rays, meet at a point as in Fig. 25, there are various results according to whether the waves arrive in phase, i.e. peak arriving with peak, or out of phase, i.e. peak arriving with trough, or intermediately. When the two sets of waves

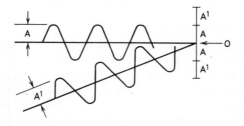

Fig. 25. Interference

arrive in phase the amplitude of one is added to that of the other, resulting in enhanced brightness. When the sets of waves arrive out of phase a peak of one is cancelled or reduced by the trough of the other, resulting in zero or reduced amplitude, i.e. the brightness is diminished. When this occurs, the waves are said to be out-of-phase by 180° or half a wave-length, assuming that a complete cycle from wave to wave is regarded as 360°. Intermediately, if the waves arrive out-of-phase by less than 180°, various degrees of reduced brightness are the result. This phenomenon is known as interference.

Retardation

If we have two parallel rays of light, completely in phase, i.e. peaks level with each other, and we pass one ray through air and the other through a transparent substance such as glass, the ray passing through the glass is delayed, or retarded in relation to the one going through air. The amount of retardation depends on the optical density and thickness of the glass. As will be seen from Fig. 26, the peaks of the second ray, on emerging from the glass,

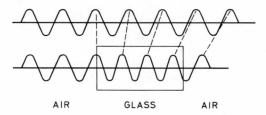

AIR   GLASS   AIR

Fig. 26. Retardation

are now behind those of the first one in air, so that the retardation has altered the phase relationship between the two rays. Note that both density and thickness cause retardation.

Direct and Diffracted Rays

Suppose that in a microscope field we have a very small specimen, almost a dot, with a clear surrounding area. As light passes near the specimen it is affected according to whether it passes through the object or through the surroundings. In the latter case, the light takes a certain path through the microscope, and we call these rays the direct rays (Fig. 27). But the light passing through the object itself is scattered by the object and takes a quite different path, almost as if it had passed through a lens. We call these rays the diffracted rays.

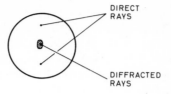

Fig. 27. Direct and diffracted rays

Image Formation

These diffracted rays are retarded in relation to the direct rays according to the optical density difference between the object and its surroundings, and also by the thickness of the object.

The two sets of rays, direct and diffracted, eventually meet at the eyepiece where they interfere with each other, producing brightness, shade, or darkness according to the phase-relationship between the two sets of rays at the point of meeting. Thus the microscope picture which we see is, in reality, a very complex interference pattern, for the results of light going through one point of an object, as in the case just considered, are repeated by light going through every other point of the object.

The strongest CONTRAST between the object and its surroundings is obtained when the direct and diffracted rays arrive at the point of interference out of phase by about one half of a wave-length. Then, provided that the amplitudes are the same, the result will be no light, i.e. darkness, due to 180° out-of-phaseness. But, as the object consists of areas of differing thickness and/or refractive index, the amplitudes and retardation vary, and the result is a pattern of greys ranging from black to white, forming the microscope image.

Phase-Contrast

Having established the foregoing facts, we are now in a position to understand how phase-contrast is obtained. If we have a very transparent object whose density or thickness is insufficient to create a phase-difference of about one half of a wave-length between the direct and the diffracted rays, the object can barely be seen and it is in such cases that phase-contrast comes to the rescue.

7

In their passage through the microscope, both sets of rays pass through the back focal plane of the objective lens. Because of this, we have here a position at which we can apply some modification to the rays to produce certain desired results.

The light source is made in the form of an annulus, and the sub-stage condenser forms an image of this annulus at the back focal plane of the objective. At this point is mounted the *phase plate*. Essentially, see Fig. 28, this consists of a disc of glass in one face of which is an annular groove or depression. Any light passing

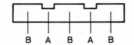

Fig. 28. Phase plate

through this groove, as at AA, has less glass to penetrate than light passing through the remainder of the plate, as at BBB. Remembering what we have learnt about retardation, we can see that rays passing through BBB, having more glass to penetrate, will be retarded in relation to other rays passing through AA.

In phase-contrast we form an image of the light source annulus at AA, the annular groove of the phase plate, and the rays producing this image are all the direct rays. The rays which are scattered by the object, the diffracted rays, will pass through the remainder of the phase plate, BBB. The retardation imposed by the phase plate, which is one-quarter of a wave-length, added to the slight initial retardation imposed by the object itself, due to its optical density and thickness, usually about one-quarter of a wave-length, amount to the desired one-half of a wave-length retardation necessary to produce an image of good contrast when these two sets of rays meet and interfere with each other. This has been achieved by retarding the diffracted rays and so altering their phase relationship to the direct rays. In other words, we have obtained good *contrast* by a *phase* alteration. Hence the name of this technique: *phase-contrast*.

As we get maximum contrast when the amplitudes of the diffracted and direct rays are nearly equal, we have to reduce that of the brighter direct rays by coating the annular groove in the phase plate with a deposit similar in effect to a neutral density filter.

Equipment

The equipment necessary, in addition to the microscope, consists of the following:

A lamp, preferably with a condenser and variable control of intensity. An annular disc in a centring mount, situated at the back focal plane of the substage condenser, or, if using the system devised by John R. Baker, the lamp fitted with condenser and centring annulus holder which produces an image of the annulus at the back focal plane of the substage condenser, exactly equivalent to the other system. A phase plate fitted into the objective at its back focal plane, each objective having its own phase plate and matching annular disc. An auxiliary telescope which is used, in setting-up in place of the normal eyepiece, to enable us to see the phase plate within the objective, not visible through the normal eyepiece, and so be able to position the image of the annulus exactly upon the dark ring of the phase plate.

Setting-up

The steps in setting-up are as follows:

1. Direct light into the microscope as near as possible to axial. By focusing the objective and/or substage condenser, view the partially closed iris diaphragm of the substage, if necessary centring this to the field and correcting the angle of light from the lamp to make it truly axial.

2. Place specimen on the stage and looking through the normal eyepiece, focus the objective containing the phase plate until the specimen is approximately in focus.

3. Remove the eyepiece and insert the auxiliary telescope. Focus the eye-lens of the telescope to give a very sharp image of the dark ring of the phase plate. Insert the annulus.

4. Focus the substage condenser to give a sharp image of the bright annulus, noting that the size of the annulus varies as the focusing of the condenser is altered. By slightly refocusing the condenser and, if necessary, centring the annulus holder, superimpose the bright annulus exactly on the dark phase-plate ring. The annulus must lie *on* the dark ring and a common mistake is to make the annulus surround and enclose the phase ring, or to make the phase ring enclose the annulus. It will be found that the width of the dark phase ring is somewhat greater than that of the bright annulus. Having got the two concentric, slightly raising or lowering the substage condenser

will control the size of the bright annulus to the exact amount required.

5. When the bright annulus is completely superimposed on the dark phase ring, the microscope is in adjustment for phase-contrast and the normal eyepiece now replaces the auxiliary telescope.

6. Make final adjustment of the focusing of the objective on the specimen. A very slight readjustment of the focusing of the sub-stage condenser may now be necessary to produce maximum contrast. Generally, with most specimens, the complete alteration in appearance when the microscope goes into phase-contrast will indicate when the adjustment is perfect, although beginners may care to revert to the auxiliary telescope to check this. With very little experience, however, this is unnecessary.

7. For changes of specimen, using the same objective, only minor changes of focus of the substage condenser will be necessary to compensate for varying thicknesses of slides. This is because for each slide thickness, the objective has to be raised or lowered to focus the object. This movement of the objective and of the phase plate which it carries has to be compensated by similar movement of the substage condenser to maintain superimposition of the bright annulus on the dark phase ring. Either the telescope may again be employed to re-establish complete superimposition or, with a little experience, the appearance through the normal eyepiece will enable the user to judge when this has been attained.

8. For a change of objective it is desirable to revert to the telescope to check both the centration of the next bright annulus and its superimposition on the phase plate of the new objective. It will be appreciated that each change of objective requires a change of annulus disc to match. Steps 3 onwards should be repeated for the new objective.

General Notes

Phase-contrast can be applied to both monocular and binocular microscopes.

The following objectives can be fitted with phase plates: achromatic series—16 mm, 4 mm and 2 mm (oil-immersion). Fluorite series—3·6 mm and 2 mm (both oil-immersion). Usually, the phase plate is built-in permanently to the objective but, in one make, the phase plate is removable from the objective so that existing objectives can be converted for phase-contrast by fitting the plate. An objective with a phase plate in position can be used for ordinary transmitted light with very little loss of performance, at least with the lower powers, but there is some little loss with the highest powers.

As usually supplied, phase plates give *positive phase*, i.e. the thicker or more highly refracting parts of the object appear dark.

Before the advent of phase-contrast, the only way to see very transparent objects in their natural living state, i.e. without killing, preparing and staining, was to use dark-ground microscopy. This technique, while it demonstrates the shape, size and presence or absence of motility of the object, shows only the outer envelope; no internal structure is visible by dark ground. Phase-contrast, on the other hand, allows us to see the interior of these very transparent objects.

CHAPTER 10

Polarized Light

Polarized light has many uses in microscopy, particularly in work dealing with crystals, such as in mineralogy, geology, chemistry and in work on precious stones. For such purposes special polarizing microscopes are used in crystal identification for the measurement of angles and for studying colour effects. At such level the work forms a study in itself, and there is considerable literature covering the subject.

For students, however, particularly in biology, and in medical laboratories, there are simple uses of polarized light, and this chapter is intended for such students as an introduction to the principles involved, and the application of these principles to simple microscopes. For any more advanced information, the reader is referred to the special literature and catalogues of equipment.

Polarized Light

Light is generally defined as a form of energy proceeding from point to point along straight lines, but travelling in a series of waves at right angles to the direction of travel. This is illustrated in Fig. 29, OO being the axis along which the light is proceeding and AB the height of the waves above and below the axis line. As drawn in

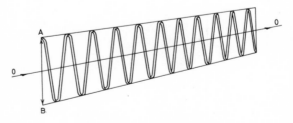

Fig. 29. Light propagation

the diagram, the waves are in the plane of the paper and, if we could look along the axis from O to O, we would then see the waves in the vertical plane (see Fig. 30). However, light vibrates not only in one plane but in all planes simultaneously. Consequently there

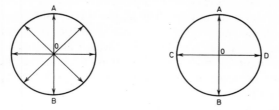

Fig. 30. *Axial view of unpolarized light*

are planes of waves at all angles, two of which have been drawn in Fig. 31. This kind of light is called unpolarized light and is the type found in ordinary daylight, lamplight, etc. Let us consider two such

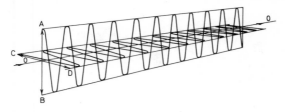

Fig. 31. *Two planes of unpolarized light*

planes AB and CD at right angles to each other, as indicated in Fig. 32. They proceed along the axis OO until something causes some change. If we imagine a kind of grid or filter, PL, with parallel

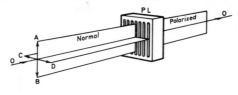

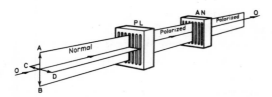

Fig. 32. *Polarizer produces polarized light*

bars and slots, interposed on the axis of the light, and so positioned that the slots are vertical, then the vertical vibrations or waves will pass through PL quite easily and will emerge on the other side. The horizontal waves cannot get through the vertical slots, and they are stopped and do not emerge. The grid which produces this effect is termed the "polarizer", and the light which does emerge is termed "polarized light", which, therefore, may be defined as light which vibrates in one plane only as distinct from unpolarized light which vibrates in all planes.

Let us suppose that another grid or filter, AN, is now placed on the axis of the polarized light. Provided that the slots are placed vertically, in the same plane as the polarized light, the light will pass through without difficulty and continue towards O as polarized light. This second grid is termed the "analyser". If however,

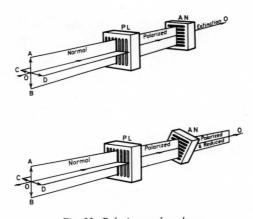

Fig. 33. Polarizer and analyser

the analyser is set so that its slots, or to use the correct term, its axis is at right angles to the plane of the polarized light, then, as there are no horizontal vibrations to go through the horizontal slots all the light, which is vibrating vertically, is stopped and no light will emerge, and we get extinction.

Intermediately between these two positions of vertical and horizontal axis of the analyser there are angles at which some of the vertically polarized light can just manage to pass through, but such light will emerge still polarized, but considerably reduced and, of course, the closer the axis of polarizer and analyser come to being parallel the greater will be the amount of light which will pass through the system.

Whilst most transparent substances will transmit polarized light without any alteration of the plane of vibration (or the plane of polarization), there are certain substances which are able to twist the light around its axis as it passes through them. Such substances are called "bi-refringent" or "optically active". In Fig. 34, the unpolarized light reaches the polarizer PL with its axis, say, vertical. Vertically polarized light emerges and would be stopped by the

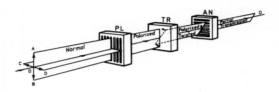

Fig. 34. *Optically active object*

analyser AN if the axis of the latter were at right angles, horizontal, to that of the polarizer. If an optically active substance, TR, is placed between the polarizer and the analyser, the vertically polarized light will be twisted as it passes through TR and some of this modified light will get through the analyser. The emerging light, although reduced in intensity, will be quite visible.

Some optically active substances are: crystals of all kinds; starches; cuticles of leaves and bulbs; natural fibres of cotton, wool, silk, flax, hemp, and most animal hairs; some man-made fibres; fish scales; thin sections of horn, hoof, claws and nails; decalcified bone; muscle fibres; certain oils and fats.

Polarizers and Analysers

Without going into the complex optical reasons responsible for the effect, it can be accepted that certain crystalline substances possess the ability to filter out from unpolarized light all planes of vibration except the one which lies on the optical axis of the substance. Until recent times, by far the commonest was Iceland Spar, which was cut in a certain way and mounted, to form the so-called "Nicol Prisms". A pair of such prisms, suitably mounted so that one lay between the source of light and the object under examination, and the other between the object and the eyepiece constituted the polarizer and analyser system of all polarizing microscopes. In their mountings provision was made so that the axes of the prisms could be set in relation to each other, and, when these axes were at right angles, light was extinguished and a black field presented through the eyepiece. This represented the ideal set-up, for against this black field any optically active substance, situated between the polarizer and the analyser became visible as a bright object, usually coloured.

More recently, owing to the difficulty in obtaining supplies of suitable Iceland Spar, an alternative has been used—Polaroid material. As with the Nicol prisms, Polaroid will filter out all planes of vibration except that in line with the axis of the Polaroid, thus providing the source of polarized light. However, when the axes of two pieces of Polaroid are crossed, there is not a black background, as in the case of Nicol prisms, but a background of some colour, ranging from a deep magenta to a deep blue, depending upon the quality of the Polaroid. Generally, the contrast between the bright optically active substance and this coloured background is sufficient to show the former quite clearly. There are limitations imposed by the coloured background of the Polaroid in certain work in crystallography which is more advanced than the work discussed here.

With the addition of simple polarizers and analysers, any ordinary microscope can be used for simple work with polarized light. The polarizer is usually a disc of Polaroid material mounted between two thin glass discs, to protect the rather delicate Polaroid against scratches, and made to fit the filter carrier of the substage. The analyser is usually another disc of Polaroid, similarly sandwiched between thin glass discs and mounted as a cap over the eyepiece. It can be freely rotated and locked in any chosen position.

Using Polarized Light

In the simplest uses of polarized light such as are being considered, the chief purpose is to show the presence or absence of some optically active substance, not normally visible or identifiable when using ordinary unpolarized light. Having focused the objective of the microscope with the axes of the polarizer and analyser parallel, one or the other is then rotated until the darkest possible background is obtained, even if, with Polaroid, this is coloured. Against this background, any bright or coloured detail can be said to be the image of some optically active substance.

In some of the medical applications, the following are typical examples:

Particles of silica in lung tissue, in silicosis.

Particles of asbestos in lung tissue, in asbestosis.

Particles of mica in post-operative tumours, e.g. in a talc granuloma.

Particles of starch in post-operative tumours, e.g. in a starch granuloma.

It should be stressed that such simple polarized light microscopy does no more than show the presence of optically active material, but, with two exceptions, it is not possible to identify the material by name, although the size and shape may assist in the confirmation of a diagnosis in a suspected case. For instance, asbestos, if suspected, can usually be confirmed by the parallel fibre structure generally visible in even tiny fragments and, often, by the frayed out fibrils at the ends of pieces of asbestos.

Maltese Cross

The two exceptions mentioned above are starch and perspex dust. In both of these substances, in addition to the bright and/or coloured appearance of the particles when viewed through crossed

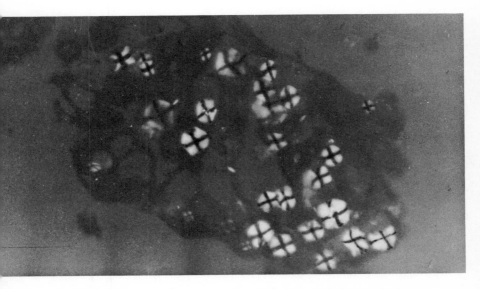

Fig. 35. Starch in a granuloma, by polarized light, showing the Maltese Cross

polarizer and analyser, each particle displays a black Maltese Cross over the particle.

The photomicrograph shown in Fig. 35 is of a starch granuloma and it will be seen that each tiny particle of starch displays this black cross either perfectly or partially. At one time it was thought that this appearance was specific to starch, forming a positive identification, but, recently, some workers have shown that finely divided perspex particles display the same appearance.

CHAPTER 11

Fluorescence Microscopy

This chapter is intended for students as an introduction to a comparatively new technique which is being rapidly developed in certain work in medical and in industrial applications. It is not proposed to do more than state the principles involved, the type of equipment required, and the use of such equipment in a simplified form on standard microscopes.

Definition

Fluorescence is a phenomenon displayed by certain substances whereby, if they are illuminated or irradiated with short-wave light, (ultra-violet), they are able to convert the short-wave light which is invisible, into long-wave, visible light. This long-wave visible light persists only as long as the substance is being irradiated by the UV in the case of true fluorescence. It can happen, however, with certain substances, that the induced visible radiation will persist for some time after the removal of the exciting UV, and in this case the phenomenon is termed "phosphorescence".

Fluorescence—Primary and Secondary

There are many natural substances, particularly of a botanical and of a mineralogical nature which, without any preparation, display fluorescence in colours specific to the substance when irradiated by UV. This natural fluorescence is termed "primary fluorescence" and has been known for some time.

When investigations were made on other substances of zoological and medical interest, results were disappointing. A certain amount of fluorescence was seen, but the intensity of the visible radiations was very low and there was no specific coloration to enable differentiation to be made. An Austrian worker then discovered that other substances, mainly certain dyes, themselves showing primary fluorescence, and which he named "fluorochromes" could be applied in very dilute aqueous solutions (1 in 1000 to 1 in 10,000) to various tissues in similar manner to biological staining, and that, as they were specific to various tissues, such tissues could be demonstrated by the fluorescence of the fluorochrome attached to them. This type of fluorescence was termed "secondary fluorescence" and has become of great importance in medicine. The fact that the dyes are used in such dilute concentrations reduces possible damage to the cells, especially living cells, to the minimum.

Fluorescence Microscopy

The two chief uses of this technique following what has been said, are:

(a) The study of substances which have primary fluorescence, as, for instance, in botany and in mycology. The appearance in fluorescence can often show differences in structure or arrangement not normally visible in ordinary transmitted light technique.

In mineralogy, various rare earths, such as cerium, strontium, thorium, etc., and minerals such as fluorspar, felspar, apatite, and uranium combinations all display primary fluorescence.

(b) The study of material by secondary fluorescence promoted by fluorochrome staining. Some of the dyes used for this are: auramine, analine blue, acridine orange, thioflavin S, thiazo yellow G, fuchsin, coriphosphin O, fluorescein isothiocyanate, etc., also, amongst the antibiotics, tetracycline. The current literature should be consulted for the recent developments.

Probably the first serious medical use of this technique was the use of auramine as a stain for tubercle bacillus in sputum. Taking this as an example, each organism becomes visible as a luminous yellow rod against the dull or black background, and it was claimed that, when there were only a few organisms on a slide, a much higher count was obtained because of the increased visibility of the organism as compared with the usual Ziehl-Neelson staining.

Further applications have followed, and two currently used ones may be mentioned:

(1) The acridine orange (A.O.) technique for the detection of very early malignancy. This depends on a change in the RNA of the nucleus of a malignant cell. This change alters the fluorescence of a normal nucleus from a yellow-green to a flaming orange colour, and it is claimed that earlier identification of malignant cells is thereby obtained as compared with the more usual staining technique.

(2) The antibody tracer technique, also called Coon's technique, has many variations at present under investigation. The principle is

to make antigens visible by labelling with a fluorescent dye the antibodies reacting with these antigens. As immunization is concerned basically with the formation of antigen specific antibodies, the ability to see and count the antibodies is invaluable, and there is a vast literature available on the subject to which any interested reader is referred.

Equipment Required

In ultra-violet microscopy the use of glass is prohibited, as glass is opaque to the short wave-length UV which is used in this work, and quartz must be used. Fluorescence microscopy is different in that it uses the longer wave-lengths of the UV spectrum, and at wave-lengths around 3500 Å, at which the fluorescing dyes and materials are quite active, optical glass will pass sufficient UV for the purpose, thus avoiding the need for very expensive quartz lenses, slides and cover glasses.

The intensity of the fluorescence depends on the intensity of the UV which is irradiating the material. In the auramine T.B. technique it is possible to obtain sufficient UV from a tungsten lamp of, say, 100 W to cause the auramine to fluoresce. But while this fluorescence is just about enough to make the organisms visible, a much higher intensity is really required.

The first requirement, therefore, is a source of high intensity UV, and the most convenient source is the high pressure mercury discharge lamp such as the 250 W ME/D lamp (Mazda, and others) or the German lamps HBO. 200 W, or C.S. 150 W. Such a lamp is mounted in a well ventilated lamp house equipped with a glass lens condenser system, and, sometimes, a metallic reflector to send the back-emerging rays forwards towards the condenser.

As all these lamps emit UV, heat and visible light, a system of filters has to be used. Many preparations used in fluorescence microscopy are wet preparations, and the heat must be eliminated by a heat-absorbing filter, such as the ON.22 (Chance).

Next, the visible light has to be removed. There are various combinations of filters for this, and two simple ones will be described: (a) A Wood's filter, OX.1 (Chance) is transparent to UV which it transmits, but it is opaque to visible light except the very long wave-length of ruby light, and also the infra-red, which are both transmitted. The older system used a liquid filter (4 % ammonium copper sulphate) not less than one inch thick, to remove both the ruby light and the infra-red rays—thus producing a dark background.

(b) In more recent times, and to provide a good dark-ground effect without the trouble of using a special dark-ground condenser the OX.1 filter is followed by an "interference filter". This filter cuts the wide UV spectrum down to a narrow band at 3650 Å at which wave-length optical glass is comparatively transparent and fluorescing materials quite active. This filter is opaque to the visible wave-lengths, except deep blue, and this residual colour effectively neutralizes the red which would be transmitted by the OX.1 filter, thereby producing a dense black background.

Finally, a very important filter has to be used. After the UV has irradiated the fluorescing material, its work is done and it has to be removed, for prolonged exposure to UV light can cause serious damage to the eye. To safeguard the user, a "stopping filter" or "UV suppression filter" is used. Such a filter is the OY.12 (Chance) which is quite opaque to UV. It can be fitted anywhere beyond the specimen—behind the objective, or in the body of the microscope, or inside the eyepiece, the latter being a very usual position. Certain objectives, particularly the fluorites and the apochromatics which incorporate fluorite in their construction, can display primary fluorescence when irradiated by UV emerging from the specimen, particularly if observations are being made under bright-field conditions as opposed to the dark-ground conditions produced by the filter systems first described. In these cases, a special protective front glass, opaque to UV is mounted over the front lens of the objective (Leitz) or an UV absorbing cover-glass is mounted over the specimen.

Given the suitable filter system, the microscope can be any ordinary microscope. Certain modifications can be made to improve the supply of UV to the specimen and to increase the brilliancy of the fluorescence. If a mirror is used to direct the UV into the condenser of the microscope, there will be some absorption of UV if a glass mirror is used. Substitution by a surface aluminized mirror is recommended for this purpose. While all sub-stage condensers will transmit some UV, the more complex ones with multiple lenses and cemented components will absorb more UV than very simple condensers with single lens elements. The use of the simple student Abbe condenser, with two air-separated lenses has been found to be quite effective.

In many of the techniques the intensity of the fluorescence is low, and the emitting areas are very small. If a binocular head on the microscope is replaced by a monocular head, there is an increase of more than double the intensity of the fluorescence. Similarly, the use of low power eyepieces, ×4, ×5 or ×6, is advocated, as the image brightness is inversely proportional to the square of the power of the eyepiece.

Further, in view of the low intensity of many fluorescing specimens, maximum contrast will be obtained by screening daylight and room light from both the microscope and the operator, either by working in a dark room or cabinet, or, as a minimum, by providing a dark hood or screening box to cover instrument and operator. For similar reasons, especially when using simple lamp arrangements which are not built into the microscope, there should be adequate screening of the visible light coming out of the lamp house on to the bench and surrounding walls—but this should be done without any interference of the adequate cooling of the lamp house. This is most important.

Setting-up

Assuming that work is to be done with simple equipment, additional to and external to a standard microscope, Fig. 36 shows

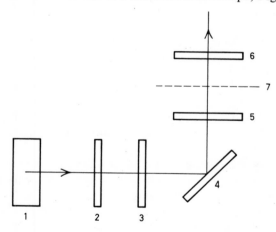

1. MERCURY DISCHARGE LAMP
2. HEAT FILTER, ON. 22
3. INTERFERENCE FILTER
4. SURFACE ALUMINIZED MIRROR
5. WOOD'S FILTER, OX. 1
6. STOPPING FILTER, OY. 12
7. OBJECT PLANE

Fig. 36. Order of filters for fluorescence

the position of the various units. The following procedure should be carried out under such circumstances:

1. If the lamp is not of the instant-starting type, it must be switched on and allowed to work up to operating intensity for some 15 min before being used. Note that with this type of lamp, any interruption of the supply current, even momentary, as by a faulty connection or accidental switching off, will extinguish the lamp and it cannot be relighted until the mercury vapour has condensed back into liquid mercury, a matter of some 12–15 min, after which the heating up has to be repeated.

2. Insert the "Stopping Filter", OY.12, in the eyepiece or other position. If in the eyepiece, unscrew the cell of the eye-lens and drop the filter into the eyepiece to rest on the diaphragm.

3. Insert the heat filter, ON.22, in the lamp house or anywhere between the lamp and the microscope.

4. Focus the lamp condenser to produce an image of the flame of the lamp on the mirror of the microscope.

5. Insert the "Woods filter", OX.1, usually in the filter carrier of the substage.

6. Place the specimen on the stage.

7. Using the red light from the Woods filter, OX.1, adjust the mirror position, focus, and, if necessary, centre the substage condenser to produce maximum illumination in the field of view.

8. Focus the objective still using the red light.

9. Introduce either the copper sulphate filter or the interference filter at any convenient place between the lamp and the microscope, but after the heat filter—see Fig. 36. This will produce the dark background against which any fluorescing material will be seen.

As all stray fluorescence must be avoided, great care must be taken to avoid any grease, which is fluorescent, on the mirror, substage condenser, slide or cover-glass.

As most oils are fluorescent, use of the oil-immersion objectives calls for a special non-fluorescing immersion fluid. A non-fluorescing liquid paraffin has been used, but most workers use a specially prepared fluid—"Fluorfree Immersion Fluid" (Gurr). In connection with this last one, it has been noted by some workers that prolonged exposure to light will make even this fluid fluorescent, and it should, therefore, be stored away from light until it is actually required.

The foregoing description of equipment and procedure covers

the simplest accessory-type; various makers, especially on the Continent, have produced complete and complex microscopes for fluorescence microscopy in which the illumination is built into the stand of the microscope, and in which there are easily interchangeable filters to produce various combination results. There is also a large and growing literature on the whole subject of fluorescence microscopy.

CHAPTER 12

Photomicrography

It can be taken as an axiom that, if an object is visible through the eyepiece of a microscope, it can be photographed. The quality of the photograph depends primarily upon the optical characteristics of the microscope; these, however, must be assisted by the best possible system of illumination to bring out these characteristics to the maximum. The camera, strange to say, plays the least important part, being, in essence, merely a holder for the photographic material—plate or film.

Photomicrography is achieved by projecting an image from the eyepiece on to the sensitized photographic material. As in all projection work the intensity of illumination falls off rapidly as the projection distance is increased—the "inverse square law" operates, so that by doubling the projection distance the illumination is reduced to one quarter. Hence, in order to have enough light for accurate focusing, and, also, to reduce exposure times to reasonable dimensions to avoid, for instance, fogging due to vibration, a fairly powerful light source is generally required.

Microphotography

To clear up a common confusion of terms, it can be stated that while photomicrography is the art of producing by projection through a microscope, a large picture of a very tiny object, microphotography is the reverse of this, that is the production of a very tiny photograph of a very large object. In this latter technique the object, e.g. a picture or a book page is strongly illuminated and is set at the plane of focus of the projected image of a microscope. The light travels through the microscope from the eyepiece to the objective which focuses an image, very much reduced, on to photographic material. This results in a photograph so small that it has to be viewed through a microscope to become visible. A common exercise, when this technique was in fashion, was to produce a photograph of the Lord's Prayer in the form of a dot, smaller than a pin head. During the second world war, considerable use of this technique was made by the intelligence services on both sides, in producing the "micro-dot" method of communication. The micro-photograph of a letter, list, or plan was reduced down to the size of a full stop or comma and then inserted in written material such as an addressed envelope or a letter whether hand-written, typed or printed made no difference. As, of course, a microscope is necessary to read the micro-dot, "agents", or spies to whom the dots were sent, were equipped with a collapsible microscope to give a magnification of $\times 200$.

Simple Photomicrography

At its simplest, photomicrographs can be obtained by projecting an image from the eyepiece on to a piece of bromide paper, pinned flat at right angles to the projection direction. Screening of the paper from accidental light is, of course, essential, but quite usable photographic records have been obtained in this manner.

Magnification

In all projection work the magnification of the final image, whether on a screen, or bromide paper, or a film or a plate, depends on the distance from the eyepiece to the screen, etc. The total magnification of the microscope, i.e. objective magnification multiplied by eyepiece magnification is repeated at a projection distance of 10 in. At any other projection distance, the screen magnification is modified by the ratio of 10 in. to the actual projection distance. For example, if the total magnification of the microscope is $\times 200$, the screen magnification for various projection distances are given in the following table:

Projection Distance (in.)	Screen Magnification
10	$\times 200$
3	$200 \times \frac{3}{10} = \times 60$
5	$200 \times \frac{5}{10} = \times 100$
15	$200 \times \frac{15}{10} = \times 300$
20	$200 \times \frac{20}{10} = \times 400$

Projection distance is the distance from the eye-lens of an eyepiece to the actual screen, etc.

Eyepiece Disc Photography

An unusual, but quite effective method has been demonstrated, in which advantage is taken of the fact that at the diaphragm inside the eyepiece, an image of the object is formed by the objective prior to subsequent magnification by the eyepiece. The microscope is set up in the ordinary way to give the most perfect image possible. The illumination is then extinguished or blocked off and the eyepiece is removed and taken to a dark-room where a disc of photographic film is dropped on to the eyepiece diaphragm after the removal of the eye-lens. Having reassembled the eyepiece (the eye-lens will prevent the eyepiece from falling down into the body of the microscope) it is shielded from light and taken back to the microscope and inserted in the body. Exposure is made by switching on the light or removing the obscuring block. Again, with safety precautions, the eyepiece is taken back to the dark-room and the film removed and developed. Naturally the photograph is very small but it should be quite sharp. Its magnification will be that of the objective only, and usable prints can be obtained by the use of an enlarger.

Box and Miniature Cameras

It is possible to secure photomicrographs by applying a box camera or a miniature film camera, complete with its lens, as close as possible to the eye-lens of a microscope which has been focused previously for visual work. The camera lens must, however, be focused for infinity before use. Exposure is made by use of the camera shutter. Needless to say the camera must be held rigidly over the microscope during the exposure. The resulting photograph is generally a small disc but it is capable of enlargement to a reasonable degree.

Eyepiece Cameras

This type of camera has become very popular in recent years. This is due partly to the very small space on the bench required to enable good quality photomicrographic work to be done, and partly to the big increase in colour photomicrography. As the cost of colour materials is still very high except in the 35 mm size, a great number of workers have adopted the 35 mm camera in eyepiece form, for this work.

As usually arranged, the camera is clamped to the top of the microscope body above the eyepiece. *A beam-splitting prism*, either permanently mounted, or removable by a swing-out action, is set above the eyepiece. As shown in Fig. 37, the beam splitter consists of two prisms cemented together, but the cemented face of one of them is semi-silvered, i.e. it is covered with tiny specks of silver with clear spaces in between them. According to the relative areas of silver and clear spaces, controllable in manufacture, the ratio of light passing through the prism to the light reflected sideways from

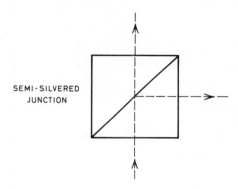

Fig. 37. Beam-splitting prism

the silvered areas can be adjusted to various needs. Often the ratio is 50–50, but in some cases the side-reflected light is 30% and the transmitted light 70%, and so on.

The reflected light is taken to the viewing eyepiece which is fitted with a graticule, while the transmitted light travels on to the plate or film.

The beam splitter is followed by a timed shutter, and at the top of the camera is the body carrying either a plate or a roll of film. Figure 38 shows an eyepiece camera with the viewing eyepiece and a film body on a standard microscope.

In use, as all focusing is indirect, or by transfer, it is very essential to eliminate parallax due to personal accommodation of the eye. (See Chapter 7, where a similar problem exists.) The correct procedure with this form of focusing is to put the microscope objective out of focus. Then focus the eye-lens of the viewing eyepiece very carefully to make the markings of the graticule, usually a central cross, as sharp as possible. When, following this, the objective is brought into focus, whatever is in focus in the viewing eyepiece will be equally focused in the camera. The position of the object to

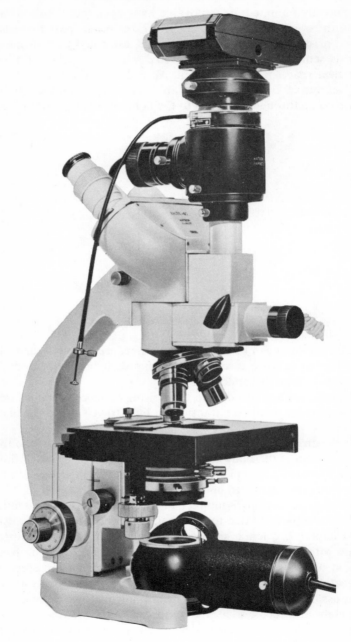

Fig. 38. Eyepiece camera on microscope

be photographed can be adjusted at this stage. Usually, the graticule carries additional marks defining the coverage of a frame of the
35 mm camera, or that of the plate if a plate body is being used.
With focusing and positioning completed, exposure is made.

Extensible Bellows Cameras

Many of the classical photomicrographs have been taken on
this, one of the oldest forms of the photomicrographic camera. It is
made either on a long horizontal bench or in vertical form to be
set up above a vertical microscope. In the former set-up there is
virtually an optical bench carrying, in sequence, the illuminant, the
lamp condenser, filter holders, the microscope placed horizontally
with the mirror removed, and the camera which is fitted with long
extensible bellows and with interchangeable ground-glass focusing
screen and plate-holders, usually of $\frac{1}{4}$ plate size, but, sometimes, as
large as $\frac{1}{2}$ plate. In the vertical form, the light is directed on to the
mirror of the microscope, which is vertical, and the camera is
mounted on a separate vertical pillar and base, so that there is no
physical contact between the camera and the microscope. Again,
this camera has extensible bellows and removable focusing screen.
As this screen is horizontal, and usually rather high, a 45 degree
mirror is often supplied, to stand on the focusing screen and allow
the operator to stand normally before the microscope and avoid
having to climb up to see the screen.

In both of these cameras, the advantage of the bellows is that,
with a given set of objectives and eyepieces on the microscope,
intermediate magnifications are obtainable by extending the bellows—and, hence, the projection distance—so that the whole
photograph covers only the part of the specimen in which interest
is centred, and, further, as focusing is directly on the screen, there
can be no errors of parallax.

Focusing Screens

Any camera which depends upon focusing on a ground-glass
screen, such as the bellows cameras just mentioned, or some of the
smaller reflex cameras now in use, is a little difficult to use because
of the diffusion of the image on the screen due to the grain size of
the grinding. A tiny dot on the specimen will be shown as a small
disc on the screen and focusing has to be judged by the reduction
of such a disc to its smallest possible diameter. Users differ in their
ability to judge the exact point of focus by this method, and the

alternative, a clear glass screen, is to be preferred, once the worker has become familiar with its operation. As a clear glass screen is not always readily obtainable, some workers convert part of the ground glass to clear glass by cementing a small cover glass over the centre of the ground glass. The action of the cement and cover-glass is to remove the effect of grinding and to present a small area of clear glass through which the final focusing is done.

In use, there has to be an additional piece of equipment—*the focusing magnifier*. This is a small magnifier with a flat base which is applied to the screen, and with a focusable eye-lens. Prior to use, it is set on a piece of ground glass, or an exposed photographic plate, on the side away from the ground surface, or the emulsion surface, and accurately focused for the user (this is an individual or personal adjustment) until detail of the grinding or of the emulsion is seen. A pencil mark on the ground surface, or on the emulsion, is of help for this. The focusing adjustment is then locked with the clamping ring provided, and the magnifier is ready for use. With the clear glass screen in position on the camera (or with the focusing magnifier over the cleared patch on a ground screen) an aerial image projected from the microscope eyepiece is examined through the magnifier whose base is in contact with the screen. As there is no diffusion from the screen, it is possible to see the image in sharper focus and so facilitate perfectly focused images in the camera.

Illumination

Photomicrography of good quality and with the minimum of trouble is achieved by the use of light of sufficient intensity and controlled to produce the maximum efficiency from the optical system of the microscope.

Köhler illumination is, therefore, the best possible form, and the reader is referred to Chapter 5 where the technique and necessary equipment are described. All that is said there applies equally to photomicrography except that, as we are dealing with a projected image all adjustments and observations are made on the screen or in the viewing eyepiece. Exact centration throughout the system is most essential, and this can be checked by focusing the objective and/or the substage condenser until images of the substage iris diaphragm are clearly seen. The lamp iris diaphragm and the light source itself are focused in succession on the centre of the screen or of the viewing eyepiece without any further adjustments of the centring. Failure to do this usually results in a shadow or some uneven illumination on one side of the photograph often not visible until after the photograph has been developed.

While medium and high-power photomicrography are fairly easy, using such critical methods, low-power work causes much more difficulty in filling the field with even illumination. Every advantage must be taken of the use of either low-power substage condensers, if available, or of the removal of the top lens component of a standard condenser. Further, some lamp systems incorporate an auxiliary lens which can be brought into position to modify the original lamp condenser and so fill the field with even light.

Light intensity can present a problem by being too low for easy focusing, or too high, causing dazzle during focusing, and some method of modifying the intensity must be employed. With too low an intensity, assuming that the optical system is correctly set-up, the only remedy is to use a source of greater intensity, although it should be remembered that early photomicrography of great quality, including work on diatoms and bacteria, was achieved with the light from an oil lamp! Many of the modern lamps have means of controlling the intensity either by a rheostat or by a stepped transformer. For visual work, focusing, etc., the light can be reduced to a comfortable level, but it is always advisable to photograph with the light at maximum intensity. This is for two reasons: (a) with a constant intensity, one of the variables affecting exposure time has been eliminated, (b) in colour photography, the colour-temperature of the light source is of importance in the rendering of true colour, and most lamps have a colour-temperature of around 3200 °K, the ideal for this work, when working at their full rated voltage.

The addition of Neutral Density Filters can effect a reduction in intensity, but in colour work there is a difficulty—see the section on Filters below.

Whatever system is adopted for light control, the worker MUST NOT do anything by way of de-focusing of condensers, or over-closing of iris diaphragms for this purpose, otherwise the critical optical set-up will be disturbed with resulting inferiority of the photomicrograph.

Macrophotography

This form of photomicrography at magnifications of × 12 downwards, is often the most difficult to manage. The combination of the lowest powers of objective and eyepiece, say × 4 with × 4, results in a total magnification of × 16, which is too high for the purpose. If the eyepiece is omitted, it is possible to reduce the projected image to a little more than × 4, but this is usually accompanied by drawbacks in the form of scattered light due to internal reflections in the microscope body, and cut-off, reducing the size of the field covered, due to the comparatively small diameters of the body and eyepiece tube. Moreover, as has been discussed in Part 1, there are certain types of objectives which require the eyepiece to help in their corrections (see p. 30).

A very satisfactory method exists if a bellows camera or its equivalent is available. At the front of the camera is mounted a so-called "photomicrographic lens" which is built like a camera lens, say an anastigmat, with a built-in iris diaphragm to control the depth of field. Such lenses are made by Wray, Watson, Leitz (Summar) and Zeiss. The microscope is removed and, in place of it, is some simple device which will hold a slide at right angles to the axis of the camera. Behind this device is the illuminating system suitably modified in its condenser by the use of a special low-power or macro condenser to fill the field with homogeneous light. It should be noted in this set-up, that instead of attempting to produce an image of the light source or of its diaphragm on the specimen (such an image will generally be too small to cover the field), as is normal practice in photomicrography, the light should be so focused that an image of the source would be produced within the photomicrographic lens itself. Under these circumstances the object lies within a solid cone of homogeneous light and it is photographed in quite uniform illumination. Photomicrographic lenses have been made with focal lengths of 3, 2 and 1 in. Using the 3 in. lens, with the camera bellows closed to the minimum, a screen magnification of from × 2·5 to × 3·5 is usually possible, with a specimen coverage of up to $1\frac{1}{2}$ in. diameter. Increase of bellows length, i.e. of projection distance, raises the screen magnification accordingly. The *copying camera* is usually quite suitable for this class of work, without alteration of the camera, but with the addition of the slide holder as described above.

Exposure Times

The length of exposure depends upon a number of variables, namely, the thickness and density of staining of the specimen; the speed of the photographic film or plate; the intensity of the light; the total magnification of the microscope; the numerical aperture of the objective; the projection distance. The fewer the variables, the less error is likely in judging the correct exposure, so that the standardization of conditions as far as possible is an obvious first step. There will remain some variables outside the control of the operator, and it is because of these that either additional equipment, or the past experience of the operator becomes essential, if loss of time and of photographic material is to be avoided. Despite the apparent difficulties, it can be stated that a comparatively short experience of the equipment and of specimens of similar nature does enable an estimation sufficiently close to exact timing, to be made of the correct exposure time merely by looking at the focusing screen or through the viewing eyepiece. Naturally, photographs which are very largely a repeat of some similar subject are easier to estimate, especially if, and this is recommended as standard practice, a full *log book* is kept of every exposure made. The log should contain details of objective, eyepiece, screen magnification, light intensity, photographic material type, speed of the material always expressed in the same notation, e.g. A.S.A. number, nature of the specimen, the staining of the specimen, any filters used, the exposure given and the final result, e.g. perfect, over-exposed, under-exposed, etc. *Every* exposure should be recorded, including failures, for we can learn a lot from our mistakes.

Apart from personal estimation, instrumental help is available, and there are on the market various *exposure meters*, some of them adaptations of ordinary exposure meters for general photography, and others which are specially developed photo-cells and meters or recorders. Provided that they are sufficiently sensitive to the comparatively low light intensities met in photomicrography, any of these are suitable, but the user should be on his guard against such meters which give only a small scale deflection when exposed to the light from the microscope. With such small deflections, it is not possible to judge exposure times correctly.

Many workers advocate the use of *test exposures*, especially when working with new equipment or on strange specimens. A few frames of film at different exposure times can usually indicate the correct exposure, while, if a plate camera is in use, a series of strips of the plate can be exposed for varying times by the gradual withdrawal of the slide between each exposure.

Colour Filters

Except in colour work, almost all photomicrography is best done with the use of some appropriate colour filter. The purpose of the filter is to emphasize some detail in the specimen, or to suppress uninteresting detail, in other words, to promote the greatest possible contrast in the photograph. The choice of filter depends on the colours in the stained specimen, the detail which is of most importance, and the nature of the film or plate. A further benefit from the use of filters, even with unstained objects lies in the fact that, as photographic plates and films are more sensitive than the eye, small colour errors—chromatic aberrations—which are not fully corrected in achromatic objectives are recorded as out-of-focus fringes, marring the sharp outlines. Using monochromatic light, as is obtained using a colour filter, eliminates the residual chromatic aberrations and makes achromatic objectives perform very much better as a consequence.

There are two types of filter available, the Wratten type which is a sheet of coloured gelatine sandwiched between glass, and the solid coloured glass type as made by Chance. While there is a rather larger range in the Wratten type, many workers prefer the solid glass, remembering that where there is a concentration of high intensity light there is a similar concentration of heat, and the heat can damage the gelatine but not the glass. Because the filters affect the amount of light available to the camera, they affect the exposure time, and each filter has an "exposure factor" attached to it. This means that if an exposure time for white light has been established, the time has to be multiplied by the appropriate factor to give the new time when that filter is employed. The Table gives a list

Table of Filter Factors

Colour	Code No.	Factor
Ruby	OR.1	× 80
Red	OR.2	× 4
Deep orange	OY.1	× 2·5
Orange	OY.2	× 2
Yellow	OY.3	× 1·5
Light green	OY.13	× 2
Green	OGr.1	× 6
Blue green	OB.2	× 6
Daylight blue	OB.8	× 3
Blue	OB.10	× 50
Purple	OV.1	× 250
Neutral	ON.10	× 14

of the Chance filters and their factors which are correct for slow or medium speed panchromatic films or plates; other types require some variation of the factor, which information is usually available from the maker.

It was stated, above, that these filters are used in black and white work and not in colour photomicrography. This is obvious as the colour of the filter would spoil the natural colour of the specimen, but some workers have used the neutral filter, ON.10, in the above list to modify the light intensity in colour work, and have been disappointed in the result, finding that a greenish tint overlies all the photograph. This is due to the fact that the neutral filter does not reduce the intensity of all colours equally, and transmits more of the green part of the spectrum than other wave-lengths. In view of this, other means to control light intensity in colour work are to be preferred to the use of this filter.

The Automatic Camera

Where personal estimation and judgment are involved, errors can arise, and it would seem that a photomicrographic equipment which could adjust itself to varying conditions would be ideal. Such equipment is now on the market, and while it is expensive, it does remove much of the work from the user, who has little more to do than select the field of view on the specimen and press a button.

One such automatic equipment is the "Orthomat", by Leitz. This is a complete photomicrographic unit, with illumination built into the microscope, adjustable for either transmitted or incident light techniques, provision for continuous binocular viewing of the specimen, and an automatic film camera. The operator selects the film speed, the magnification and the part of the specimen to be photographed, and then presses a button. The machine measures the light intensity, adjusts the exposure time, makes the exposure and winds on the film to the next frame.

Such an instrument has obvious advantages in establishments where large numbers of photomicrographs of widely varying specimens have to be undertaken. There are several others by various makers, but they are, essentially, as described.

Polaroid-Land Camera-Back

One further development must be mentioned, the adaptation of the Polaroid-Land camera-back to the eyepiece camera for photomicrography. This system, developed in America, provides a positive paper print within seconds of making the exposure without any of the intermediate steps of developing the film to produce a

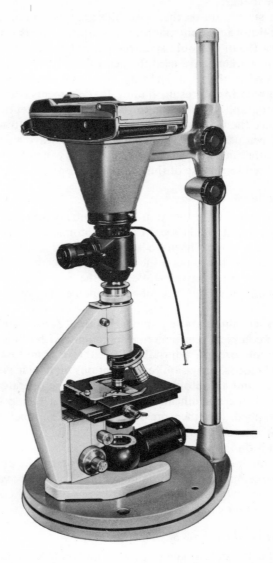

Fig. 39. Polaroid-Land camera-back on eyepiece camera

negative, making a contact print from the negative and processing the print.

One such adaptation is made by W. Watson & Sons Ltd., and Fig. 39 shows the Polaroid-Land camera-back applied to the Watson eyepiece camera on a standard microscope provided with a self-contained Köhler illumination unit.

The Polaroid-Land film is supplied in a sealed roll and is loaded into the camera. It contains its own processing materials and, after making the exposure, a knob is pressed and a strip of paper pulled out of the camera. After a pause of some 10–20 sec, the back of the camera is opened and the paper positive is removed. The only additional work is to coat the print with the special glazing fluid provided with the film, and a permanent positive print results.

As only one print is obtainable from each exposure, and there are no negatives as such from which other contact prints can be made, repeated exposures must be made if a number of prints of the same field are required. The print size is $3\frac{1}{4}$ in. $\times 4\frac{1}{4}$ in. (82 mm $\times$ 108 mm) and the magnification factor of the camera is $\times 1$ resulting in a print magnification equal to the total magnification of the microscope.

One great advantage of the system is that it is possible to check immediately that a perfect photograph has been obtained, without disturbing the particular field of the specimen which, once moved, may be very difficult to find again. Another advantage lies in the availability of very high speed films. Whereas an average panchromatic film has a speed of, say, ASA.125, the ordinary Polaroid film is rated at ASA.200. But for cases of low light intensity, such as incident light photomicrography in metallurgy, fluorescence microscopy, multiple filter work or the recording of moving objects, there are available films with speeds of ASA.3200 and even ASA.10,000, thus reducing to reasonable dimensions the very prolonged exposures normally necessary with very low light intensities.

In addition, there is one variety of film with a speed of ASA.800 which will produce not paper prints but black and white transparencies for projection, size $2\frac{1}{4}$ in. $\times 2\frac{1}{4}$ in., and one additional type which will produce prints in colour.

It would seem that the absence of dark-room facilities, and of the knowledge and of the materials required for photographic processing are no longer a bar to the production of good quality photomicrographs. Anybody with a microscope and a camera of this type can produce them quickly on the bench.

CHAPTER 13

The Stereoscopic Microscope

With any microscope hitherto described the image seen is a flat picture, possessing length and breadth but no appreciable depth. Yet, in nature, if we view any object with our two eyes, we are able to see and to judge this third dimension of depth, without which the full appreciation of the shape of things cannot be realized. Such binocular vision is termed "stereoscopic vision" and it is based on the fact that, because our eyes are separated by an appreciable distance, each eye sees the object from a slightly different angle, and other objects nearer to or further away from the eye have different relative positions to the object being viewed. In average persons the inclination of the axes of the eyes when viewing an object at the normal near or reading distance is approximately 15°.

At this point it should be made clear that not all binocular microscopes can produce stereoscopic vision. Those described earlier in the book present to the two eyes identical images of the object on which the microscope is focused, the output from the objective being divided by a beam-splitting prism and presented equally to both eyepieces. This happens whenever a single objective is in use.

In the stereoscopic microscope we have, in effect, two complete microscopes, each with its own objective and eyepiece, and, as the two microscopes have an inclination separation of 15°, the images presented to the eyes differ, as they do in normal unaided vision, and a true stereoscopic picture is seen, having length, breadth and depth—the so-called "3D" picture of today.

There is a vast field where a certain amount of magnification, coupled with true stereoscopic vision, can be of use in the examination and manipulation of small objects. Some uses of the stereoscopic microscope are: small dissection of plant or animal tissues; judgment of the shape of bacterial colonies; examination of small surface detail in metals, textiles, paper, wire, etc.; examination of the interior of wire-drawing dies, including diamond dies; small

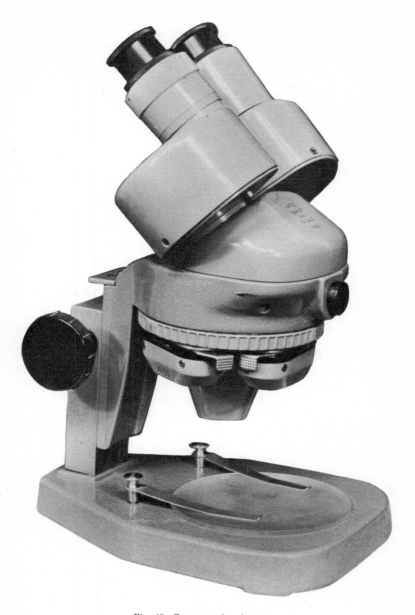

Fig. 40. Stereoscopic microscope

assembly work such as transistors; inspection of finished parts, raw materials and checking of flaws and defects.

For such work certain conditions are essential: a flat field of view, as large as possible; a long working distance to accommodate tools and instruments during dissection, assembly or manipulation; and good optical qualities to provide clear images free from distortion of shape and colour, and, for every magnification, the maximum depth of field, consistent with the maintenance of these other essentials. It follows, therefore, that the optical parts of a stereoscopic microscope differ from those of conventional microscopy, and they are specially calculated and made to provide these essential requirements. A further difference between conventional and stereoscopic microscopy is that, in the latter, the images are erect and not inverted, making movement and manipulation very easy, and everything is seen in its natural sense and position.

Figure 40 shows a typical stereoscopic microscope. In common with every microscope of this type it has the optical head which carries, at its lower end, the twin objectives, in this case covered with a shroud for protection. (In this particular instrument there are three pairs of objectives, which will be further described under the heading of *Magnification Changers*.) Above the objectives are duplicate prism systems which make the image erect instead of inverted, and which provide inclination of the eyepieces to a comfortable working angle. Above the prisms are the tubes to take the eyepieces, and they are separable to accommodate the varying interocular distances of different users, and one tube has adjustment to alter the focus to compensate for any differences of focus between the two eyes. The whole system from objectives to eyepieces is set at a converging angle of 15°, thus providing, in effect, two complete microscopes set at that angle, thus providing for stereoscopic vision.

Magnifications. Size of Field. Working Distance

These three features are inter-related and play an important part in the usefulness of a stereoscopic microscope. The range of magnifications is lower than is usual in conventional microscopy, so that the stereoscopic microscope fills the gap between the simple hand lens, say × 2·5, and the lower powers, say × 60, of the conventional microscope. The details in the following tables are quite typical, and are taken, with permission, from literature provided by W. Watson & Sons Ltd.

Stereoscopic Tables

Magnification

Objectives	Eyepieces			
	× 5	× 7	× 10	× 14
× 1·25	6·25	8·75	12·5	17·5
× 2·5	12·5	17·5	25	35
× 5	25	35	50	70
× 10	50	70	100	140

Free Working Distance

Objective	Working Distance
× 1·25	85 mm (3·35 in.)
× 2·5	74 mm (2·91 in.)
× 5	42 mm (1·65 in.)
× 10	22 mm (0·87 in.)

Field of View (Diameter)

Objectives	Eyepieces			
	× 5	× 7	× 10	× 14
× 1·25	22·0 mm (0·87 in.)	22·0 mm (0·87 in.)	19·0 mm (0·75 in.)	13·5 mm (0·53 in.)
× 2·5	10·0 mm (0·40 in.)	10·0 mm (0·40 in.)	9·2 mm (0·36 in.)	6·6 mm (0·26 in.)
× 5	5·0 mm (0·20 in.)	5·0 mm (0·20 in.)	4·6 mm (0·18 in.)	3·3 mm (0·13 in.)
× 10	2·5 mm (0·10 in.)	2·5 mm (0·10 in.)	2·3 mm (0·09 in.)	1·6 mm (0·06 in.)

Magnification Changers

Various devices are employed by different makers for the easy change of magnification. In the instrument illustrated in Fig. 40, there are three pairs of objectives mounted on a rotating turret or nosepiece, and movement of the latter to a new position, indicated by a locking spring plunger locates the next power of objective. In another make, the objectives are mounted on a rotating drum. In another there is a built-in system of auxiliary lenses which are interposed between the objectives and the eyepieces to alter the total magnification. In all cases, the magnification can be increased to varying degrees by the substitution of different powers of eye-pieces.

Mountings

As was said earlier, all stereoscopic microscopes have in common the optical head with its focusing mechanism. Thereafter, there are a great many different forms of mountings ranging from the simplest stand with the specimen on the bench, through various forms of platforms or stages to hold the specimen for either transmitted light or incident top lighting, or both, to special mountings to hold the microscope in position on a machine or similar applications. The mounting range is such that it is usually possible to find a suitable mount for almost every form of work.

Accessory Equipment

Illumination, often of variable intensity, can be provided for both top lighting of variable obliquity, and for bottom or trans-mitted light. Micrometer eyepieces with graticules (Watson and others) provide for simple measurement and comparison of size. A movable stage (Watson), polarizer and analyser (Watson), dark-ground illumination (Watson) and eyepiece camera photography (Watson) are amongst other available accessories which extend fur-ther the usefulness of this very valuable microscope.

The Zoom Stereomicroscope

In the stereoscopic microscopes first described, changes of mag-nification, by whatever system, are effected in fixed steps. There is need, on occasion, for magnification, between limits, to be con-tinuously variable, and this is provided in the recently developed Zoom Stereomicroscope (Watson, Bausch and Lomb, Zeiss).

The Zoom system was originally developed by W. Watson & Sons Ltd. from the work of their Dr. Hopkins, for the television camera. In essence, one has a lens system whose focal length, and, hence, magnification, can be altered continuously, between certain limits in the order of 3:1, or 5:1 in the current Watson model. During changes of focal length, the focus of the lens system remains constant, only the magnification and the field coverage being altered.

The following description is of the Watson 5:1 Zoom Stereo-microscope (see Fig. 41). As will be seen from this diagram, the optical system consists of the objective lenses, the prisms, and the

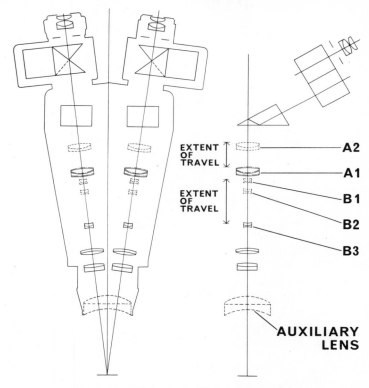

Fig. 41. Optical diagram of Zoom stereomicroscope

eyepiece lenses on axes converging at 15°, as in the usual stereo-scopic microscope, but with the addition of a lens system of variable position interposed between the objectives and the prisms. Changes of magnification are effected by an intricate mechanical gear which gives a complex movement to the elements of the Zoom system, as is indicated by the various A and B positions in the diagram.

Externally, the microscope differs in having a box-like structure below the prisms, as shown in Fig. 42, which houses the lens system and the mechanical parts of the Zoom elements.

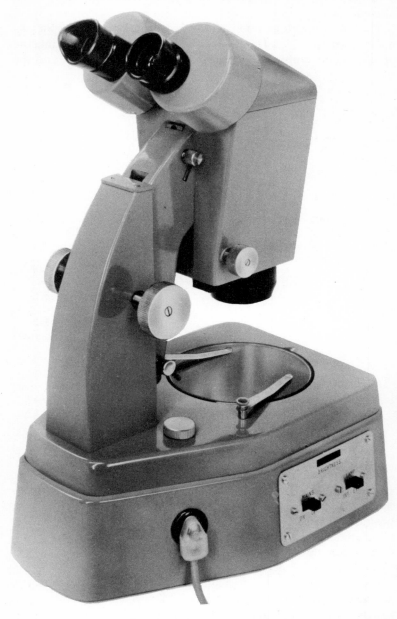

Fig. 42. Zoom stereomicroscope

In this illustration the large milled head controls the focusing; the smaller head at the side of the Zoom box controls the Zoom range of magnification change, and there is a small indicator located on the top of the Zoom box to show how much of the Zoom range, which runs from 0 to × 5, is in use. As illustrated, the base incorporates the illumination system for either top or bottom lighting, with variable control of intensity.

Magnification

The objectives are of fixed power and the total magnification can be varied by changes in eyepiece power, by use of the Zoom control and by the addition of one of two auxiliary lenses below the objectives. As a result, a wide range of magnifications is available, together with the accompanying changes of fields of view and working distances. The following table shows this range:

Table of Zoom Range Data

Wide Angle Eyepieces	Auxiliary Lens	Magnification Range	Field of View Dia. (mm)	Working Distance
× 10	—	× 10 − × 50	20·0–4·0	78 mm (3·1 in.)
× 10	× 0·7	× 7 − × 35	28·5–5·7	78 mm (3·1 in.)
× 10	× 1·5	× 15 − × 75	13·3–2·7	33 mm (1·3 in.)
× 15	—	× 15 − × 75	13·8–2·8	78 mm (3·1 in.)
× 15	× 0·7	× 10·5− × 52·5	19·7–3·9	78 mm (3·1 in.)
× 15	× 1·5	× 22·5− × 112·5	9·2–1·8	33 mm (1·3 in.)
× 20	—	× 20 − × 100	10·3–2·1	78 mm (3·1 in.)
× 20	× 0·7	× 14 − × 70	14·8–2·9	78 mm (3·1 in.)
× 20	× 1·5	× 30 − × 150	6·9–1·4	33 mm (1·3 in.)

As with all other stereoscopic microscopes, the images are erect, and the converging eyepieces are inclined at an angle for comfortable operation, having, also, an adjustment for inter-ocular distance, and compensation for differences in focus between the two eyes.

Using Stereoscopic Microscopes

In setting-up these microscopes, the width between the eyepieces should be correctly set so that the operator sees both pictures equally. If there is any optical difference between the eyes, one of the objectives should be focused on to an object with one eye, the eye above the adjustable eyepiece being kept closed. After careful focusing, this eye is then opened and the other closed, and, if the image is not as sharp as before, rotation of the eyepiece adjustment should be done to make this so.

As all magnifications are low, they are quite controllable by coarse focusing only, and only one control is provided.

Eyepieces and objectives are always parfocalled, that is, after focusing with any combination of eyepiece and objective, other eyepieces and objectives can be brought into use without the need of refocusing. There is one point, however, which should be noticed. These objectives have a considerable depth of focus; consequently, if initial focusing is done on a low-power objective before going to a higher power, the latter may not be in perfect focus as the original focusing may have been done not at the mid-range of depth of the low-power objective but at either the upper or the lower limit of depth. It is better to do the initial focusing through the highest power objective which has the minimum depth of focus, after which subsequent objectives will be found to be parfocal.

A final point concerns the choice of objective and eyepiece combination to produce some desired total magnification figure. As the value of the stereoscopic image lies mainly in the depth of focus of the objective and in the field coverage, and as these two features are greatest with the lowest powers of objectives, we reverse the rule of conventional microscopy (using the highest possible objective and lowest eyepiece for any particular magnification) and we choose the lowest power objective which, with the eyepieces available, will produce the desired magnification.

Suggested List for Further Reading in
FLUORESCENCE MICROSCOPY

Auramine T.B. Technique

Mackie, T. J. and McCartney, J. E., *Handbook of Practical Bacteriology*, 7th Edn., 1946, 658–659 (publ. E. & S. Livingstone Ltd., Edinburgh).

Richards, O. W., Kline, E. K. and Leach, R. E., *Amer. Rev. Tuber.*, 1941, **44**, 255.

Pathology

Gagne, F., "Review of Microfluoroscopy in Pathology", *Laval. med.*, 1963, **34**, 57.

Quantitative Methods

Donath, T., *Mikroskopie*, 1963, **18**, 7.

Ruch, F. and Bosshard, U., *Z. Wiss Mikroskop.*, 1963, **65**, 335.

Acridine Orange Technique

Bertalanffy, F. D. (from Department of Anatomy, University of Manitoba, Winnipeg, Canada), "Fluorescence Microscopy for the Rapid Diagnosis of Malignant Cells by Exfoliative Cytology", *Mikroskopie*, 1960, **15**, 3/4.

Bertalanffy, Ludwig von (from Department of Zoology, University of Alberta, Edmonton, Canada), "Acridine Orange Fluorescence in Cell Physiology, Cytochemistry and Medicine", *Protoplasma*, 1963, LVII, 1/4.

Equipment

Makers' catalogues, such as the following:

W. Watson & Sons Ltd., Barnet, Herts.. England.

Vickers Instruments Ltd., York, England.

Reichert & Co., Vienna. (Agents—Shandon Scientific Co. Ltd., London, England.)

E. Leitz & Co., Wetzlar, Germany and London, England.

Index